BOARD
ANTWAN S. TAYLOR
GAMES

Written by Antwan S. Taylor
Edited by Kendra Applewhite (www.Kymwrites.com)
Cover Design by Lee McMiller (www.LeevisionDesign.com)

For information, contact:
BoardGamesTheNovel@gmail.com

First Edition

ISBN-13: 978-0692130407

Printed in the United States of America
T.R.U.E Stories Media Corporation
Markham, IL

REMARKS FROM THE AUTHOR

Like most kids my imagination ran deep; I was infatuated with movies early on and I would create stories in my head.

Storytelling has always been my strongest attribute and that is why it brings me great joy to finally release one of my stories to the world. Entrepreneurship is a major key in the Black Community; therefore this book contains many gems in regards to that field. I put a lot of energy into this piece of work mentally, emotionally, and spiritually. I am just thankful that YOU are reading this.

Episode 116 of my entrepreneurial podcast, *Mogul Motivation*, was titled "No Way Out" it originally aired on iTunes January 3rd, 2018. In that episode, I challenged myself to finish this novel. I want to use my journey as an example to prove that no matter what you are up against no matter the circumstances you can, and will accomplish your goals you just cannot quit. Never forget that in all things with faith, WE WILL WIN

Special Acknowledgements

Words really cannot express the gratitude I have for those of you that supported my pre-order campaign. The blind faith you expressed in me will never be forgotten.

Dernea Thomas-Hall
Angela Taylor
Miracle Lilley
Tashena Briggs
Zellessia Ejalonibu
Tiara Kilgore
Susie Brown
John Jeffrey
Leah Jacob
Zeinob Amoo
William Gettings
Micah Gettings
Allatwon Jackson
Yahya Muhammad
Kourtnee Nealy
Natasha Bates
Brittani Berkeley
Leah Langley
Tyler Colson
Latrice Lawson

Ashley Harris
Latisha Pettis
D'ontae Valentine
Sherri Johnson
Kriss Shelton
Darryl Chavers Jr.
Heather Owens
Keandra Johnson
Mariah Wilkins
Brandee Neal
Shaun Johnson
Vashaun Hale
Manushka Gracia
Marquetta Johnson
Terelle Hampton
Shannon Flanagan
Bernard Muhammad
Edward Follins
Jessica Campbell
Andrea Brewer

DEDICATION

This book is dedicated to my grandmother Lillie Mae Robinson &
my uncle Ronnie Robinson. Who both shared my love for movies
and a great story. May they both Rest in Peace. No matter what
else happens I fulfilled my promise to you two. And lastly but
not least, my mother who raised me on her own. I have yet to
meet anyone that matches her perseverance and I never will.

When history was rewritten, it would start with him.

CHAPTER 1

"WHAT DRIVES YOU?"

MARCUS DREER LOVED TWO THINGS: winning and payback. The sparkles from the Patron bottle illuminated the small VIP section, where he watched Carter and his friends rejoice.

Carter was just the average Joe, enjoying a good time with his friends on a Thursday night in early June. They decided to check out Dreams Lounge & Grill, a small yet respectable lounge on the outskirts of Chicago's South Side in Markham. The lounge sat on the corner of a small strip mall that was nearly deserted with the exception of Lil Carl's chicken joint.

Dreams stood above the other neighborhood bars. It had a touch of class to it. Small in size, the lounge's dance floor space was approximately two-thousand square feet with cocktail tables spread throughout. There were two small VIP sections available—one near the front and one near the back by the restrooms. Dreams' amenities and elegance made up for its lack of space.

The server made her way to Carter's table, which put a smile on his face. Already drunk from the previous bottle, Carter spilled his drink as he stumbled over to her.

"Damn, another free bottle. You so kind to me," he said, his words slurring together. "How about you take my number down and we link up when you off or something?"

The server just smiled at him as she walked away. Carter and his companions overindulged on the tequila. He didn't know why he was receiving such presidential treatment—free VIP along with free bottles. He dared not to ask questions. He planned to ride this wave out until it was time to go.

Unbeknownst to Carter, Marcus watched him from across the lounge floor. His entire five-foot seven inches frame stood motionless. While growing up, people joked about him dressing up like T.I. for Halloween because of their strong resemblance. But on this night, he dressed like the Grim Reaper in his black slacks, black loafers, and unbuttoned black shirt.

His focused, calculated eyes became more intoxicated as he observed the people in VIP. A quiet rage burned in him as he approached the section. He walked stride for stride, his smooth light brown hands clasped behind his back; no one interrupting his course as his hazel eyes remained fixed on his prey.

"Everyone enjoying themselves tonight?" Marcus asked in an enthusiastic tone as he made himself comfortable in the VIP area. A visibly drunk Carter focused his eyes on him.

"Marcus? Marcus Dreer is that you?" Carter asked.

Marcus nodded, confirming his identity. "How's life?"

"Man, what's up bro?" Carter extended his hand to dap Marcus. "Life is good, can't complain. I'm working at this warehouse out in Joliet making a good twenty-two dollars an hour. I'm a supervisor. About to move into this house with my baby mama and shit! I can't complain at all. What about you?"

"Oh. That's nice." Marcus nodded, as he rolled up his sleeves. "What are y'all drinking?"

Carter attempted to pass him a cup. "Shit, some Patron. This is the third 5th they brought over. You trying to hit this?"

"Nah I'm fine, thank you though." Marcus sat down and stared at Carter for a moment, stroking his goatee. "You remember that time in college when we were at the Union Party freshman year and you tried to stunt on me?"

Carter sat his drink down and frowned in confusion. "What?"

"Yea, I remember it like it was yesterday. You told me you would pay me eight hundred dollars cash if I hollered at some random girl there with her ass hanging all out. You flashed the money in my face and everything. I believe the words you used were, *if you pull her, I'll give yo ass all this cash*," Marcus recounted. "That wasn't the only time your arrogance showed, but that incident does stand out. Your whole crew was there laughing and shit."

"I don't know what you talking about fam."

Marcus pointed his finger at his foe. "You see, the point is you wanted to stunt on me. You wanted to make me look bad. You wanted to make a joke out of me. I guess cause you sold weed on campus, you thought you was Pablo Escobar or some shit?"

"You really tripping over some shit from college my nigga?" Carter fired back.

Marcus sat back in the love seat, crossed his legs, and calmly looked at Carter.

"So, you asked what I do for a living now? Well I'm a businessman. I own this lounge, I own this property, and I own that bottle you're drinking. I'm happy to see you're enjoying yourself, but I know you didn't order it. Or any of them for that matter."

"Nah, we didn't. Your people brought them over here."

"I see. Well, you know those bottles are one hundred and twenty dollars apiece. You do know that, right?"

"I'm not paying for this shit. Fuck outta here!" Carter dismissed Marcus with his hand.

"Why not? You drank it, didn't you? You said so yourself… life is good. I'm sure you got money. I'll just have my server bring your tab over."

Carter raised his voiced. "I just told you…I'm not paying for this shit! We didn't even order it."

"But you drank it, Carter. You know what you did. What's the issue, huh?" Marcus slapped his thighs. "You can't afford it? It's just three hundred and sixty dollars."

A slight look of embarrassment came across Carter's face, showing Marcus' words had hit a nerve. Carter's friends stayed quiet during their entire exchange out of shock.

Carter sighed. "Man look, how can we settle this?"

"You can pay for those bottles, or they will escort you out and have the police come." Marcus motioned to four large security guards, known as the UnderDogs, who walked up behind him. The largest of the group and head of the detail EC—nicknamed after his hometown of East Chicago, Indiana—had an intimidating presence. His dark-skinned biceps bulged through his shirt. EC stood tall at six feet six inches and weighed two-hundred eighty pounds of pure muscle.

Marcus leaned in toward Carter. "Just be honest with me. Can you afford these bottles? Yes or no?"

A shaken and disturbed Carter answered reluctantly. "No..."

Marcus stared at him for a few moments before responding. "Thank you. Don't worry about it homie. You and your friends can continue to enjoy yourselves. I'll gladly send another bottle over if you want." He stood and left the VIP section, followed by his security.

"Let's go man. Time to fucking go!" Carter told his friends as he threw the glass to the ground, shattering it into tiny pieces.

Marcus stood with his hands clasped behind his back just as Carter and his friends headed toward the door. He informed his lounge manager, Sherri, he was leaving for the night. As he exited the lounge, a moist wind blew while clouds amassed in the night sky. He felt good despite the incoming storm.

Marcus decided to head to the casino, but he wanted to change his clothes first. He hopped into his 2014 silver Chevy Tahoe and drove off. Within five minutes, he pulled into the driveway of his two-bedroom ranch style home in Markham, a southwest suburb on the outskirts of Chicago. The predominantly Black working-class city had fallen deeper into despair over the years. His home and entire subdivision were built in the late 1950s. He kept the house in tiptop shape and up-to-date. The open concept interior gave his home a modern atmosphere. He never aspired to live in a huge home, so he made this house his sanctuary.

After Marcus changed clothes, he waltzed into the home office extension in the backyard, or his 'de-facto man cave' as he preferred to call it. Whenever he wasn't at the club or casino, he was busy planning his rise to the entrepreneurial mountaintop in his personal space.

He unlocked his safe box and pulled out four hundred dollars in cash, his gambling budget for the night. He glanced over the bills that covered his desk. His modest living worked to his benefit because if he had expensive taste, he wouldn't be able to afford it.

Marcus Dreer was a subtle beast. He didn't smile much. His serious face contributed to the slight wrinkles in his forehead. Women constantly told him he was too attractive to look so mean, but in reality, he was always focused on elevating his financial status. He dropped out of Eastern Illinois University after his sophomore year after suddenly losing interest in school. He scrapped all plans of earning his degree and chose to work for himself instead—and that's what he'd been doing ever since.

Marcus acquired the strip mall and took out a business loan, turning the corner storefront into Dreams, while the two center storefronts remained vacant for a long time. Ever since he opened Dreams, the lounge kept him afloat. As a result, his business paid for itself and helped him pay his personal bills, but beyond that Marcus was broke. He didn't complain much about this out loud; he just remained focused on how to get better. The main goal was to provide a financially free life for himself and his younger brother, Malik. They only had each other, as far as family was concerned. Marcus was solely responsible for paying for Malik's education.

Whatever Malik's scholarships didn't cover, Marcus made it a priority to pay for the rest.

His best thinking happened at the craps table, or a chessboard, but tonight he felt adventurous. Marcus was not an avid gambler, but he enjoyed it as a leisure activity. Frugal at heart, he always had a set budget when he walked in and stuck to it by placing minor bets that could last the entire night. The craps table was much like entrepreneurship—every toss was a risk and there were only two outcomes, win or lose. It was a creed he lived by every single day. He voluntarily journeyed into the dark and ugly. The biggest risk he had taken in his life, perhaps ever, was already underway.

Marcus hit the expressway just as the rain began to fall harshly against the roof of his truck. He still continued to cruise at 80 mph. Marcus felt invincible tonight; he felt *good*. He'd just turned thirty-two on May 30th, and he fought for everything he had now. It wasn't much, but he was proud. Things would change tomorrow though, as he planned to take a huge leap of faith.

"Still Po' Pimpin" by Do or Die filled the interior of his car, and he dashed through the storm.

Marcus walked into the Rosemont casino as if he owned the place and ordered a Remy double from the bar before heading straight to the craps table. As he waited for his turn to shoot, he placed side bets. An attractive woman caught his eye from across the table. She was about five feet six inches with large dark-skinned breasts that commanded his attention as they spilled halfway out her red dress. Her long black flat twist hairstyle complemented her physique. The two locked eyes, and her smile warmed him even more than the shots he threw back. He motioned her to come closer. As she made her way over to him, he admired her entire body.

"Hello. You requested me?" She gave him a huge smile.

"Hey. Yes, I did. I didn't want to lose my spot in the rotation, but I would love for you to keep me company. I saw you staring at me over there." He flashed a flirtatious smile at her and extended his hand.

"I'm Marcus."

"Nice to meet you, Marcus. I'm Elise."

"Likewise. So, Elise, you here alone? Where your friends at?" Marcus looked around for strangers possibly acquainted with her.

"I'm actually from out of town. I'm here for a bachelorette party, but everyone tapped out early. I'm not sleepy, so I'm down here looking for some fun."

"Where you from, Elise?"

"Houston."

"Houston. That's what's up. I've never been there." Marcus sipped his drink and stared deep into her eyes. "Well, this is my city and since your friends can't hold their liquor, I'll take care of you for the night. That is, if that's ok with you of course."

"It sounds good to me."

When it was Marcus' time to shoot, he hit his point and cashed out. He and Elise were at the table for about two hours having a great time, drinking constantly, and laughing. She was easy to talk to, and Marcus liked that. He needed that. Elise invited him back to her hotel room once they had enough of the craps table. It was clear she didn't want the night to end. Neither did he.

As the two stumbled drunkenly into the room, Marcus looked around in amazement at the suite. He had never stayed at the casino.

He sat down in the chair next to the bed. "Well, this is nice. So, who is getting married? I never asked."

Elise pulled off her shoes. She grabbed a bottle of Honey Jack Daniels, walked over to him, and sat on the edge of the bed. "One of my friends. Her fiancé lives here. He's some big shot executive for a real estate company, and she's moving in with him after the wedding." She handed him an empty glass and poured them both a glass of whiskey.

"Tell me Marcus, what else should I know about you besides the fact you're an entrepreneur? We talked so much, but you still seem like a mystery. I mean, granted we just met tonight, but still."

"Well, what else would you like to know? I'm an open book."

"What drives you?"

"Ambition," he answered without hesitation.

Elise studied his face. "I don't believe you. Ambition for what exactly?"

"Why you don't believe me? My ambition to win in all things drives me."

"I think it's something else inside of you that's driving you. Something silent. Deadly," she whispered in a seductive voice.

"And how did you come to that conclusion?"

"I have two degrees in psychology. I'm kind of good at reading people."

"Maybe you're right, maybe you're not."

Elise giggled. "Well, here's a toast to ambition then."

The two touched glasses and took a few sips. Immediately after their toast, Elise sat her glass down, mounted onto Marcus' lap, and kissed him. Marcus, initially caught off guard by her aggression, squeezed her thighs and butt and picked her up. He laid her on the bed as he pulled her thong down and indulged his tongue between her thighs. It was a night of hot passion, and Marcus enjoyed every minute of it.

He woke up three hours after the tryst. Elise was sound asleep. As he began to get dressed, she stirred awake.

"I'm sorry, I didn't mean to wake you."

She rubbed her head. "You're good. I have to get up soon anyway. It's going to be busy today with all of these bachelorette activities."

"Sounds exciting. It's a busy day for me too. A big day at that."

Marcus buttoned his shirt and smirked at her. "You're not hung over, are you?"

"Nope, I'm fine. I just wish I could have another hour or two of sleep. What about you?"

"Yea, my head is slightly banging. I guess I had one too many drinks last night."

"Mmmm, so you're a lightweight, huh?"

Marcus put on his shoes. "You got jokes I see."

"So, will I ever see you again Mr. Businessman?"

"If you want to, you will. Like I said, I haven't been to Houston yet, so now I have a reason to go."

"Well, if you ever make it, let me know. You have my number."

"Will do, lovely." Marcus kissed her forehead. "Enjoy the day."

After he left, Elise sprawled across the bed and thought about her passionate night with Marcus. She enjoyed his company and wanted to see more of him in the future. Elise knew one thing for sure. This wouldn't be the last time Marcus Dreer laid eyes on her.

After Marcus changed clothes for the second time in ten hours, he was on the move again. He was headed downtown this time. Marcus parked his car in the parking garage and paid his fare. He stopped in the local 7-Eleven to grab a donut and coffee and then headed to the fourth floor of the Harold Washington Library where he retreated to a quiet corner. He pulled out his laptop and studied some spreadsheet accounts before checking his bank account balance. He observed the available balance had just over thirteen million dollars in it. He leaned back and stared at the computer screen initially shocked at the number on the screen. Then, a sinister smile crossed his face as he realized his plan was now in motion.

CHAPTER 2
"OUR SHIT."

VINCE BROWN'S BLOOD BOILED ON the inside as he sat there with a blank expression on his face. He was just passed up for another promotion at WestGate Financial, one of the largest financial management companies in the Midwest. Vince started his career at WestGate in middle management right out of grad school seven years prior.

"Let's take a walk," Mr. O'Sullivan said. Vince, still expressionless, followed his immediate manager out the conference room.

I worked my ass off year after year, and these bastards still don't appreciate me.

"I admire you, Vince. I do. You're one of the brightest minds we have here." Mr. O'Sullivan lightly tapped him on the back. "Truth is, we need people like you down here. If we lost you to the Executive Suite, things would fall apart. We've got good account execs and good managers, but as soon as they move to the top floor, they become lazy and only focused on those retirement checks. Then, they become politicians, got damn crook county."

Vince gave a forced, lifeless reply. "I understand…"

"I know you want it bad, so my proposition is simple. In roughly two years, I'm retiring, and you're going to be the only person I recommend to take my place."

Two fucking years! That's bullshit! I been here for almost eight, and I haven't moved anywhere. In two years y'all can fucking fire me.

Vince had vision. Since he'd been with the company, he had dreams of financing and rebuilding impoverished neighborhoods with predominantly Black residents. Gentrification in reverse, so to speak. He wanted to build better communities while maintaining the Black presence there. His superiors claimed to be on board with it; however, they constantly fed him excuses. As one of the few Black employees in his department, Vince wasn't a fool. He knew they would never green light such an idea.

The meaningless new positions they gave him weren't real promotions. They just disguised it as such. After a while, he left it alone and became dissatisfied with the plan. He started actively seeking employment elsewhere a year ago but couldn't find anything to supplant his current income. He wished he could just start his own business and do his own thing, but he had a beautiful and materialistic wife—his high school sweetheart, Janelle. He also had three children, so quitting his job wasn't an option when he had a mortgage, two car notes, and three mouths to feed.

"In two years, I'll be more than ready Mr. O'Sullivan." Vince faked his enthusiasm.

"That a boy. Just hang in there. Your time is coming," Mr. O'Sullivan said, before he walked off down the hall.

Vince retreated to his office frustrated. He started thinking of a solution to his next career move. He was arguably the brightest business mind in that entire damn company, yet he wasn't valued. Vince wasn't sure if they passed over him because he was Black or because he was younger than most of his associates. Nevertheless, he was tired of it.

His phone suddenly buzzed, and he checked his messages.

Meet me at that pub on Wacker & Wabash in 2 hours. It's urgent!

His best friend appeared to have something important to tell him. Too important to discuss over text apparently, but Vince decided to meet him in two hours. He needed a drink.

Everyone had a story, and Vince's story started as a nightmare. Born as the only child to a single mother, his childhood was rough. His mom was a drug addict, and as a result, he spent many days and nights alone and hungry. He cried himself to sleep a lot. Vince had a never-ending fear of his mom not being there to pick him up after school, and most times, that fear came true. They were evicted time and time again, and he would always become the new student—something he truly hated.

Eventually, Vince's grandmother in Markham took him in, and in his freshman year of high school, he met his one true friend—Marcus Dreer. Vince turned out to be a natural athlete. He played a key role in leading his high school, East Markham High, to back-to-back state basketball titles in 2002 and 2003. Vince had numerous basketball and track scholarship offers but elected to stay close to home to attend Indiana University on a full track scholarship. His girlfriend and soon-to-be wife Janelle was unable to find decent work in Bloomington, Indiana to support their two young children, so Vince resigned from the track team due to Janelle's career struggles. He started working while he continued his studies. Vince's intellect was exceptional, and he graduated in the top ten percent of his class. He also received his MBA. Sports led Vince into business. Without that full ride, he would probably still be an average Joe in Markham.

Vince's frustration for being stuck in the corporate mud was too much to handle some days, so he went to monthly therapy sessions. It seemed like he was constantly falling short in his marriage, fatherhood, and career. He desperately needed an escape.

Marcus walked into the pub and ordered hot wings. He sat patiently for ten minutes before he saw Vince Brown's six foot four inches dark chocolate frame in a tailored gray suit.

Vince walked through the door and removed his shades once

out of the sunlight. His pearly white teeth were fully exposed in a wide smile once he saw Marcus. He walked up to him, and the two slapped hands.

Vince sat down. "What you order me?"

"Napkins."

Vince reached over and stole a wing. "You ain't shit!"

"How's the family? Especially my god-daughter."

"Vanessa is great, Victor and Janice are great, and Janelle is Janelle."

"What happened now?"

"She wants to move in to a new house. Why? I don't know. I'm trying to tell her it's not going to make sense financially, so don't let my salary fool you. It's like you have to be rich to live a poor life."

Marcus noticed the slight irritation in his voice, so he decided to get straight to the point.

"Tomorrow I will be incorporating Urban Capital. I finally got the funding."

Vince almost choked on his water. "No bullshit! You got the capital?"

"Yessir, I got all of it. The dream is real now. So, you know what's next."

"Oh, hell yea I know what's next. D.T. King is next."

"Come with me bro! I need you to join me."

"Marc, I mean it's tempting, but I can't...I can't just up and leave my job like that. Not for a startup. The kids, Janelle—"

"Why can't you?" Marcus cut him off. "You said it yourself, you hate that damn place. Vince, I need you. I can't do this without you, real shit. You're making like what, sixty-five grand there?"

"Barely sixty-two."

"I'll give you ninety, plus I want you to be a partner in the business."

"Ninety fucking grand?" Vince took another sip of water. "Wow. You not bullshitting I see."

"We talked about this all the time as kids. How we always

wanted to be rich. How we always wanted to run shit. *Our shit.* That time is now."

Vince sat there in deep thought and let out a sigh. "I always admired you bro. I've always been proud of you. You have the freedom to do the things you wanted to do. We always had common goals. I took the corporate route and you went the entrepreneur way."

Vince paused. "Fuck it. You right. Let's go over all the formal paperwork this week. I'll put in my two weeks. I'm with you Marc. Fuck it. Let's do it!"

Marcus smiled from ear-to-ear. His best friend agreeing to join him on this new venture was music to his ears.

"My man!" The two embraced, and Vince ordered two shots of Remy Martin XO. Marcus attempted to decline after admitting he was still slightly hung over.

"Nah nigga, if I'm leaving my job, you taking this shot," Vince said.

Marcus agreed. The two enjoyed the cognac until Vince retreated back to his job for his final days at WestGate.

Marcus pulled up to Dreams. He walked in and noticed his brother was not there. He sat at the bar and called him, but Malik didn't answer. Marcus began to stock beer inventory and glasses. After thirty minutes passed, Malik Dreer finally came rushing through the door.

"Bro! Bro! I know my bad."

Malik, the 25-year-old bull, was fresh out of an accelerated business program and just added an MBA to his resume. He shared the same physical features as his older brother and was slightly taller than him by an inch. However, they contrasted greatly in personality. Marcus was reserved, calculated, and serious, while Malik was energetic, social, and carefree.

Marcus continued to stock inventory. "When I made you property manager of this place, you said you would take it seriously."

"I got tied up with some friends and traffic was crazy. Last night me, Izzy, and the homies were at this party at the W. The shit was lit all night. I'm still hung over lowkey."

Marcus ignored his brother's explanation. "I called you."

"My phone died, and I didn't have my car charger. What's good Marc, why you tripping man?"

"Have a seat bro. I gotta tell you something."

Malik sat down at the bar and prepared to listen.

"Things are about to move very fast in the next few months, ok? I need you to step up and be the man I know you can be. I'm trusting you. We're all we got."

"I hear you, bro. Trust me, I won't let you down."

"You have full property management control of this strip mall. Everyone will now answer to you, and then you report to me. Tomorrow I'm incorporating Urban Capital. You will have your share, but you have to earn it. So far you did everything we agreed on, so now we just have to stay focused."

"Damn! This shit is real I see. Like this is really happening now." Malik stroked his chin. "I'm not gonna lie, I am kinda nervous."

"Don't be. This is what we were made for."

"You right bro."

Marcus smirked. "Now bust those tables down. I'm not paying you by the hour."

"We're about to be rich."

Marcus smiled at his brother to confirm his statement.

The rain created a rhythmic cadence amongst the downtown traffic. By domino effect, the weather caused a traffic jam much to William Sherman's impatience.

"Ah, what the hell?" William muttered. "How far away are we?" he asked his cab driver.

"Just a few more blocks, sir," the Cabbie responded in his deep African accent. When they finally reached the destination, William quickly gave him a fifty-dollar bill.

"Keep the change." William swung his legs out the car door, opened the umbrella, and wobbled his plump frame into a restaurant in Chicago's financial district.

William was a sixty-seven-year-old Irish man. He was mostly bald, with the exception of a few wild gray strands of hair. His peers often joked about his round belly and teased him for being nine months pregnant. He had stained white-yellowish teeth from his heavy smoking habit. However, his craving for money was greater than his addiction to nicotine. William was overly aggressive when it came to investments. He was currently the Vice Chairman and one of the eleven shareholders in D.T. King. He was running late to meet with the qualified intermediary for his latest investment exchange.

The hostess allowed him to seat himself, so he sat down at a booth in the corner near the window. He waited a few minutes and ordered a cup of tea.

Marcus slid into the seat across from him. "Green tea is much healthier than black tea I was told."

William looked at Marcus confused. "Who are you?"

Marcus went through his briefcase. "I'm just here to talk business, that's all."

"Look kid, I don't know who you are, but I'm here to meet someone very important. Can you please leave?"

Marcus ignored William's request as he looked out the window. "It's storming bad out there, isn't it?"

William stood. "Ok, I guess I'll have to alert management."

"It won't be a good day for you if I alerted the FBI and SEC about Farmer's Boys Construction LLC."

William paused in his tracks and turned around slowly. "Excuse me?"

Marcus gave him a stern look. "Let's talk business, Bill."

William reluctantly took his seat and stared into Marcus' eyes. "Who the fuck are you?" he asked.

"I'm the one who has been playing you for so long. My sources were right, you are a greedy piece of shit. Let me get this straight. You have over five shell companies all with contracts with D.T. King? Stealing money from your own partners for a quick buck? That's low."

"Listen here you son of a bitch, I will have you nailed to the wall if you want to play this game. Where is my QI Jason?"

Marcus shook his head and leaned back as he loosened the tie around his collar.

"You really are blind, aren't you? Jason doesn't exist, William. He was made up from the start. I'm your qualified intermediary. Me. I'm the one in possession of that thirteen million dollars of dirty money you were saving to clean. You're up against the wall, and I control you now. From this point on, you will do everything I say. You're going to help me take over D.T. King. It belongs to me. Or else it'll be a shame if these documents were leaked. The paper trail is deep."

Marcus placed a manila folder on the table. "Of course you can always call my bluff, but is that a gamble you *really* want to take?"

William began to sweat. "Who the hell are you?" he repeated.

"You know who I am...last name Dreer."

The color suddenly drained from William's face, his skin pale as if he'd just seen a ghost.

"It's you..."

Marcus raised his voice. "Yea, it's me. I don't want to hear any bullshit from you. You work for me now. If you go to the authorities or even say one word to Roland Thompson, I swear to God I will ruin your life."

"You really think you can pull this off jackass? Roland will bury you! Hell, I will bury you myself!" William said.

"I already pulled it off. Why do you think we are sitting here right now? You don't concern me. I beat you at your own game. You're losing. Roland Thompson doesn't concern me either. His day is coming in due time."

William sat there in silence at a loss for words as he came to terms with being blackmailed. "What do you want from me?"

"I'm sure you're aware by now you won't be getting that thirteen million back. But every month from now, you will deposit an additional one hundred and fifty thousand into this account from your companies. I want D.T. King. Not a part of it, but all of it. I'm taking it back, and this is how things are going to go."

Marcus began to lay out his plan.

CHAPTER 3
"GENTLEMEN, WELCOME TO HEAVEN!"

THE PYRAMID WAS THE MOST luxurious gentlemen's club in the entire city of Chicago, only rivaling the ones in Miami. It had the most extravagant amenities and beautiful women. Its three stories of excitement were shaped in a cube with open space in the center. The top floor housed a bachelor party with the perfect view of all the action down below, in addition to the festivities.

Rich Thompson sat in a plush leather seat, pitching his life away to secure funding for his new business, Nubian Noir.

"I bought the intellectual property to all of the designs. I own all of this one hundred percent. Now we just need to push out the manufacturing," Rich explained to two of the top Black venture capitalists in Chicago, Mr. Jones and Mr. Rush.

"It sounds good Richard, it does. But we just don't want that risk at this moment. Our focus is elsewhere," Mr. Rush said.

"Your best bet is to sell. Victoria's Secret would love this idea," Mr. Jones added. "Now did you invite us here to talk business all night, or are we going to have some fun?" Mr. Jones removed his glasses to observe a dancer that sat on his lap.

A sexy server brought drinks to the table and handed a club soda to a defeated and frustrated Rich. "No problem. I totally understand."

"Not drinking tonight?" Mr. Jones asked.

"Not drinking ever again. I'm sober now. Those days are behind me." Rich stood up and surveyed the action around him. "Gentlemen! Welcome to heaven!"

He was hosting a party for one of his friends, and he had ordered the works. The room was filled with drunk men and exotic dancers, primarily Black with a few Latinas. Party promotion was his hustle, and it kept money in his pockets.

Richard Thompson was born rich. He was the second son of Roland Thompson, and he loved having a good time. He never really had to struggle. However, he didn't identify with the Black wealthy elite. He was a rebel. He always wanted to do things his way, not his father's way. He didn't want that shadow hanging over him.

Rich pulled some strings to reserve the entire strip club for his friend's bachelor party. Nothing but high rollers were invited to keep the dancers paid. He didn't care how they made their money, as long as they *had* money. He invited Mr. Jones and Mr. Rush because they had the money to pay the dancers, but he also invited them to pitch his new venture to them.

Rich had acquired the rights to a portfolio of lingerie and swimsuit designs a few years back. He shelved it for a while because of his other countless failed entrepreneurial ventures, but about a year ago, something changed in him. He began to evaluate the value of what he had, and he knew the line would be a hit, especially within the Black women consumer market. He just needed cash to hire more designers and staff, and to invest in manufacturing—cash he didn't have.

Rich was always a fighter though. He fought his way through alcoholism and built up the willpower to resist urges, so he knew he could find a way to finance his dreams. It would just take time.

Rich poured glasses for the friends close to him and leaned back against the railing as he watched with satisfaction. A slender light-skinned beauty at five-feet four inches tall, but nearly six feet with her heels on, strutted toward him like a lioness. They locked eyes. Her ass was so round and perfect it looked fake, but it was all natural and all hers. She caught the attention of some of the guys, but they noticed she was on a mission.

When she made her way to him, she rubbed his chest lightly. "Why are you so lonely over here?"

"Just enjoying myself, laying low. Tonight isn't about me. What's your name sexy?"

"FrenchKiss," she replied. "Well, even if this isn't your night, I want to make it about you." As she rubbed his penis, she felt it grow.

Rich licked his lips. "Well, who am I to turn you down? I guess you just made an executive decision."

"Follow me, sir." FrenchKiss led him to a private room. As the two disappeared, a drunk ignorant guy turned around and said, "Man he ain't gonna know what to do with that sexy ass bitch!"

"I wouldn't be too sure about that," another guy chimed in. "That's been his girl for over a year now. How you think we got this hook up? I mean Rich got money, but he ain't got no power in here. *She* has the power."

Marcus named his new venture Urban Capital. On paper, it was a holding company with a sole purpose to acquire other firms, regardless of size. From the perspective of personnel, it was small. Vince was appointed the President position and received a nice ninety-thousand-dollar salary. He was tasked to find organic ways to grow revenue for the firm. Malik was Executive Vice President and was starting out with fifty thousand dollars a year. His primary job was to oversee the strip mall property and grow revenue. Marcus was CEO/Chairman and gave himself a sixty-five thousand-dollar salary. Although their titles were different, it was clear they were all one team, and Marcus was the driving force. Ultimately, they all had one goal, which was to acquire D.T. King Properties Inc.

Marcus was the majority shareholder at thirty-five percent, while Vince and Malik owned thirty-two-point five percent respectively. In addition to these three, Marcus hired on one office manager for admin work and other duties. Marquita Harris was previously a bartender at Dreams, but she had to quit due to her babysitter situation. She was also studying full-time at an online school. Marcus was generous enough to hire her at U.C., as she would have a lot of downtime at the office and freedom to do as she pleased. Her salary was forty -two thousand, and she was grateful for every penny.

Urban Capital's first acquisition was Dreams and Marcus' strip mall. In contrast to their small personnel, Urban Capital was a big business on paper. They had an eight-figure investment fund, thanks to William's greed, and more than enough to cover the overhead. The team settled into a small two-thousand square foot space in a high rise near the financial district. It included a welcome area, modest-sized conference room, and three private offices.

Marcus assembled the team in their conference room.

"Alright, so what are we looking at?" Vince asked.

Marcus passed out folders to each man. "D.T. King is a registered S-Corp in the state of Illinois. It's privately traded and by law it can't have no more than one-hundred shareholders, and all must be U.S. citizens or U.S. based firms."

Malik looked over the documents in his folder. "There are currently only eleven shareholders. Roland Thompson has most of the pie to himself with fifty-one percent. I have info on six other shareholders, but four of them remain a mystery. I'm still digging."

"Interesting," Vince said. "How much do we need to get our skin in the game?"

"I want to keep a low profile at first. I don't want anyone in D.T. King to know we are serious. Not yet," Marcus said. "Jay

Foster currently owns three percent of the company. He appears to be one of the less active partners. He has missed the past twelve quarterly meetings. We're going to make him an offer."

"You sure about this?" Vince asked.

"Trust me. He's small time compared to these other guys. He only has three percent of the company. They won't notice much of a difference yet, and they probably won't care."

"Well alright then. Let's get started on this right away."

"That's exactly the plan tonight. There's a networking event up north. I'm going to check it out. Rub elbows with people with money, make our presence known."

"Let's work," Vince said.

The John Hancock Center stood tall on 875 N. Michigan Ave as the jewel of Chicago's magnificent mile. D.T. King Properties Inc. occupied the sixty-fifth floor. Chairman/CEO Roland Thompson resided in the corner office. At sixty-five years old, he stood big and tall at six feet five inches and two-hundred fifty-five pounds. The former college linebacker paced his huge office back and forth as he shouted on the phone.

"No! We need that project completed by next Friday. We will not invest any more money than what we have already. I don't care what you need to do. Fire everyone if you have to, but get the shit done!"

Roland ended the call and sat in his lavish seat. He buzzed his secretary Zora and told her to order his usual lunch—a BLT on rye from an in-house restaurant. He then phoned William Sherman.

William answered on the first ring. "It's Sherman."

"Bill it's me. Listen, we have an issue with that project in Indianapolis, and we're losing money. A lot of money. Do you know what's going on?"

"I haven't the slightest idea. It could be that project manager out there. He's a rookie. He doesn't know what he's doing. It's your call, but if it were me, I would have shut it down months ago."

"I think that time has come," Roland said.

"Perfect."

"What time are we teeing off this Saturday at the course? I suggest 8:30."

"Dammit, sorry Roland. I totally forgot about that. I'm going to have to pass."

"Oh ok, too bad." Roland laughed. "I'll give you a shout next week."

"Sounds good." William ended the call.

A wave of anxiety overcame William because he knew exactly what happened with the money for that Indianapolis project. William told Roland, the project manager was extremely naïve. One of William's shell companies was milking that project dry, and no one knew it. No one except Marcus that is, and now he was in Marcus' pocket and had nowhere to go.

Meanwhile, Roland turned to his computer and proofread an email he had constructed earlier that morning to two recipients: his eldest son, Robert, the current Chief Operating Officer of the company, and his current Senior Vice President, Elliot Briggs. Roland took a sip of his brandy and pressed send with a grin, and then he kicked his feet up on his desk.

"Ugh! I can't find any heels to wear tonight," Raven Thompson complained. Raven was the youngest child of Roland, his baby girl. She got whatever she wanted, when she wanted it.

"Relax, it ain't that serious. Those are nice, stop being picky," her oldest brother Robert said. The two were shopping downtown. Robert decided to accompany his baby sister. They didn't have much bonding time, as Robert was always busy with the business and his own family.

"I guess you're right. Whatever, I'll get these. They're only four hundred dollars." Raven rolled her eyes and handed Robert the shoebox.

"This new boyfriend of yours must really have you pressed. You're going above and beyond to impress him. Who is this guy?"

"Um, what makes you think I have a man? Nobody wants me bro!" Raven smirked as she continued to browse more shoes on the shelf.

"Cause, I know my sister. Now who is he? I need to meet this dude."

"He's a good guy Rob, nothing to worry about. I'm going to invite him to dinner next week; just putting it out there."

"Ok, we shall see." Robert checked his phone. "Where is your brother?"

"No idea. Haven't heard from him since yesterday."

Robert shook his head. "This was his idea to have a sibling day, and he doesn't even show up. Typical Rich."

"Yea, but at least we're here, and it's a good thing for you cause you get to buy everything for me."

"Lucky me. We could have gone to the gun range instead, you know."

"Um why?" Raven rolled her eyes in disgust.

"Because you need a weapon to protect yourself, sis. It's a lot of crazy ass people in this world. You need to come hunting with me one of these days."

Raven laughed. "No need for me to know how to operate a gun when I have you to protect me. Why you so obsessed with guns anyway? You trying to start a revolution or something? I'm surprised Leah doesn't trip about that whole ass armory you have in the basement."

"Mmm. Hopefully it never comes to that, but we always gotta

be prepared. Us being rich means nothing. It just means we niggas that's rich."

"Oh my God, please don't start preaching this again. I know Robert, trust me. I'm very aware of the climate we live in every day in 2017, especially with that new guy in the White House. That's why I'm striving to be a judge."

"I know you know, sis. And I'm proud of you by the way, in case I didn't tell you before. Twenty-five years old, just finished year two of law school. You're the future of this family."

"Thank you! You ain't gotta remind me of my dopeness." She laughed. "But I appreciate it, bro. I do wish Rich was here."

Robert shook his head as they glided down the escalator.

"Who knows what your brother is doing right now."

The sun beamed through the floor-to-ceiling windows as Rich overlooked the skyline from his South loop loft. He gently massaged his forehead in deep thought. His girlfriend Simone Hale, aka FrenchKiss, walked up behind him topless with green lace underwear. She placed her arms around his waist.

"What's wrong, baby?"

Rich let out a small sigh. "I was supposed to link up with my siblings today, but it escaped my mind. Like I legit just remembered."

"I'm sure they will understand, but I know that's not the only thing bothering you. Talk to me."

Rich turned around, picked her up, and threw her on the California king-sized bed, giving her a passionate kiss.

"You know me so well, huh?" Rich said.

Simone smiled from ear-to-ear. "Yes, I do."

Rich rolled over beside her. "I got this new venture in mind. It's not like the other ones in the past. This one is big." He ran his hands over Simone's underwear, observing the texture. "It's a lingerie line. I already had the prototypes made and everything. I've been talking to some people; the chances of licensing it to Victoria's Secret or Nordstrom are very high."

"Wow, why didn't you tell me?" Simone asked in an excited tone.

"I'm sorry baby, I wanted to keep it under wraps until I made some progress with it. I feel like this could really be the one that takes us to the next level. I want you to model for it. I know you don't want to be at The Pyramid much longer," Rich said.

"You right, I don't. It's cool, and I make good money, but I'm ready for something different. Dancing doesn't excite me anymore. I want to do something more constructive. Whatever you do, I'll do. You're my boss."

"I'm grateful to hear that, boo. But there is just one problem though. We don't have the cash to really fuel this thing. I exhausted almost all of my options. I'm still short."

"I can help." She sat up with haste. "I have a safe with two hundred thousand dollars in it. All cash. I've been saving it for a rainy day, and this is that day."

"No, that's your money. I'm not going to waste your money on this."

"It's *our* money. And you're not going to waste it. This will work out. I know it will. You're the smartest person I know, Rich. I believe in you."

Rich humbly accepted her offer and kissed her. "Thank you, baby. I appreciate it. Well, now we are one step closer. All we need is a million dollars more."

"You can always ask your dad…"

"Hell no!" Rich stood up. "I have a better chance of asking for change on Wacker drive."

"He's your dad, Rich. I know you two don't see eye to eye on things, but it's worth a try. Just give him the business plan and talk to him."

Rich walked back to the window and fell silent.

"Promise me babe," Simone continued after an awkward pause. "Just ask him. What's the worst that could happen?"

Rich responded after a few moments of contemplation. "I don't know."

CHAPTER 4

"...THIS IS OUR BUSINESS."

"I'M TELLING YOU, WE TAKING these national!" Marcus ripped into the chicken wing he held tightly with both hands. "Best wings I've had in my entire damn life. No one else comes close."

Carl chuckled at his compliment. "I do what I can youngblood. I'm just glad to have loyal customers like y'all."

Carl was the owner of Lil Carl's. His establishment had been there way before Marcus assumed ownership of the property. His wings had been featured in the local media time and time again and were known for their tangy mild sauce that tasted better than most competitors, including Harold's Chicken and Uncle Remus.

Malik wiped his mouth and rubbed his stomach. "I can't eat no more. I'm done."

"What you fellas got planned tonight? You working the club?" Carl asked.

"Nah, not tonight. I'm 'bout to drop him off at home, and then I have portfolio work to handle. I'm most likely going to slide through to a friend of mine's house. What about you? I know y'all gonna be humping in here with the fourth around the corner."

"Mmhmm," Carl said. "Black folk starting to get lazy for the holidays. But I ain't gonna complain. I'll cook for all of Cook County as long as they pay me for it."

"Well, we appreciate you as always." Marcus slid a one-hundred-dollar bill across the counter.

"Marcus? What's this for?"

"Just a small tip to show gratitude for your years of service."

Carl motioned for Marcus to take it back. "Naw come on now. This here is too much."

Marcus and Malik prepared to leave. "Nah, it's not close to being enough. Real talk."

"Well, I appreciate it. Here's a tip for you youngsters. Don't forget to eat vegetables. Even though I fry birds for a living don't mean I underestimate the value of healthy eating."

Marcus laughed. "I'll do that."

Malik lived in an apartment in the Kenwood neighborhood with two roommates. The two brothers rode down Lake Shore Drive under the moonlight. Marcus couldn't help but to notice Malik's watch. He had been staring at it all night.

"Bulova huh?" Marcus asked.

"Yessir, I had to do it. I needed a good watch badly."

"That's like an eight-hundred-dollar watch, bro. How you come up with that? You splurged on your first pay check already, huh?"

"Nah." Malik brushed it off. "I'm saving that for a new car. Tired of pumping money into that hooptie of mine."

"Aw ok. I just wanna make sure you not getting into anything shady, that's all I'm saying, Malik. I know Izzy and your other roommate be doing that scamming shit and that's not what you need to be getting into. We're business men, not scammers."

Malik laughed. "Izzy is a valet driver. That scamming shit is a side hustle, but I agree with you. Trust me, I'm not into any of that dumb shit seriously."

"Good to hear."

A brief silence overcame the car before Marcus continued.

"Look bro, everything I'm doing is for us man. I know I may be hard on you sometimes. It's just that I want you to realize everything we want and everything that belongs to us is coming real soon. Do you believe it?"

"Of course, I do. And I'm ready for it. I been ready for it all."

"You're doing the right thing. I just need you to be patient, ok?"

"I got you bro," Malik replied.

After Marcus dropped his brother off, he decided to take Carl's advice on buying healthier food. He stopped at the Whole Foods grocery store in Hyde Park to grab a few things. He hovered through the produce section grabbing apples and blueberries, as well as a batch of kale. From his peripheral vision, he spotted a familiar face checking out at the registers. He wasn't quite sure it was her, but he left his cart behind and rushed over to the woman to confirm.

"Dezi?"

The beautiful five feet tall mocha-skinned woman with long hair instantly turned around with a look of shock on her face, as if she had seen a ghost.

"Marcus…"

Marcus and Desirè Winters were in love for as long as they could remember. Growing up in the same neighborhood, Desirè was one of only two people who understood Marcus—the other was Vince. The two made it official in high school and became a couple. They broke up six years ago. Desirè lost her drive. She felt she didn't have a true purpose outside of supporting Marcus and everyone else's ambitions while she had none of her own. She didn't blame Marcus, but she just wasn't happy with her own life.

She opted to move to New York to work for a digital marketing company and utilize her degree in some fashion. Much to Marcus' dismay and unwillingness to be in a long-distance relationship or relocate, the two decided to end it. Marcus felt a hole in his life ever since she left. They communicated from time to time, but he decided it was best he didn't talk to her at all, so he could get over her and move on. He removed her as a friend on all social media. He deleted her from his life because he had to. Now she was back, unexpectedly.

The two shared a warm embrace.

Marcus smiled. "I can't believe this. It's really you."

"It's really me."

"How are you? Why are you back?" Marcus asked. "Here let me carry those." He took the bags out of her hands.

"Family. I decided to come back home help mom out. Plus, after being out there in New York for six years, I feel like I had enough." They exited the store and stepped into the humid July air.

"How long have you been back?"

"Since last month."

"So, what's next for you? I'm sorry if I'm asking a lot of questions. I just never thought this would happen. It's been a long time."

"You never thought we would see each other again? Yea me neither, especially after you blocked me."

Marcus looked away from her in slight embarrassment. "I'm sorry. I was angry and being selfish. I got rid of my social media as a whole not long after that. I don't have anything—Twitter, Facebook, Instagram, nothing. I tried reaching out to you last year, but I see your number changed."

"Yea, I changed my number a few times since then. And I'm not on social media either. Too much of a distraction."

"I missed you." Marcus got straight to the point.

Dezi blushed. "You always know what to say to make me feel all tingly inside." She walked ahead to lead him in the direction of her car. "I missed you too, Marcus. I never would have guessed we would run into each other like this. And to answer your question,

I'm starting a non-profit organization that helps inner city girls earn scholarships. It's called Ladies Armed with Knowledge or L.A.W.K."

"That's fantastic. I'm happy you finally found something that works for you."

"I guess I have. What about you? How's the lounge?"

"Everything is going great. I actually started a new business myself. It's a private equity firm. I'm finally making a profit these days."

"I'm happy for you, Marcus. I always believed in you. Always."

The two approached her car. Marcus didn't want the reunion to end.

"I can't let you go without getting your number," he told her.

Dezi took his phone and dialed her number.

"Now you have it." She smiled at him. "I'm back home now. Don't block me again."

"I won't. I will be keeping in touch with you, and that's a fact." He put her grocery bags in her backseat. The two hugged, and Marcus gave her a kiss on the cheek.

"See you later." Dezi settled into the driver's seat.

Marcus closed the door shut and watched her drive off with mixed emotions. He was happy and excited, but he also felt a rare emotion he didn't feel often. Chills.

Rich waited for nearly forty-five minutes outside of his father's office. A part of him believed his dad kept him waiting intentionally to be inconsiderate, while the other half thought maybe he was truly busy. Nevertheless, Rich grew impatient by the minute.

Zora, his father's secretary, called his name in a soft-spoken voice. "Rich, your father said you can go in now."

Rich ascended quickly and walked into his father's office with confidence. He felt more comfortable going into a bank as opposed to this place, but he promised Simone he would try.

"Son, I'm sorry about that wait, but today has been pretty hectic. Have a seat."

"No problem at all, dad. Money first, right?"

Roland sat on the corner of his large oak desk. "What's going on?"

"Alright. Just hear me out, ok? I've been working on a business plan lately, and it's very solid. I've been talking to some people, and they truly believe I can get some licensing deals with this. I just need an investment. I own all of the rights and everything."

"Mhmmm. Let me see that." Roland motioned for the binder in Rich's hands. Roland scanned the first few pages before he closed it. "A lingerie and bikini line, huh? No thank you." Roland handed the binder back.

"Dad, come on. Why not? Look, I really thought long and hard about this. I don't want a hand out. I just need a loan. You will get everything back plus interest. Just put a number on it. That's all I'm asking."

Roland walked around. "Son, all of the money you wasted from dropping out of school and on these silly ass ideas of yours in the past amount to nearly three million. How about you pay all of that back first with interest. Otherwise, you will never see another penny of my money again. Your mother takes care of you, and if it were up to me, she wouldn't."

Rich held his head high. "I take care of myself."

Roland laughed as he sat in his plush office chair. "How? Promoting parties at these knockoff events? What about all of these other dead-end businesses you're into? Why are you here? Surely you can find a million dollars on your own, can't you? You and that, uh, stripper you got shacking up with you."

Not surprised by his father's behavior, Rich packed his things and stood up. "Thanks Roland, I appreciate that. You have a good day." He walked out.

"Close the door behind you," Roland yelled after him.

In the hallways of D.T King, Rich was fuming. His hands trembled from rage and hurt. He couldn't contain his anger anymore and kicked over a water tank. Water soaked the hallway carpet, as people looked around startled by his action. Richard spotted his older brother, Robert.

"Rich! Rich!" Robert ran after him.

Elliot Briggs, the Senior Vice President of D.T. King, peeped around the corner.

"What the heck is going on out here?"

"Family business. This doesn't concern you," Robert said. He continued after his younger brother. "Rich!"

Rich snatched his arm away from Robert. "Don't touch me."

"C'mon bro. Let's step in here." Robert led Rich into a small empty meeting room and closed the door.

"I'm sick of that man! I'm sick of that motherfucka."

"Who?" Robert asked.

"Your father. That's who."

"You mean *our* father. Look man, he just wants you to become the person he knows you can be. That's all."

Rich paced back and forth. "Well, he has a hell of a way of showing that shit. I'm out here trying to make shit happen Robert, and he has the power to help and refuses. What kind of shit is that?"

Robert sighed. "Look, I'm tired of this war between you and dad. It's been going on for too long. How about you just come work here, Rich? It's not that bad. You're a Thompson and this is *our* business. I'll find a position that suits your needs and wants. You won't even have to deal with him at all. Just report to me."

Rich took a seat across from his older brother as he gained his composure. He looked Robert in the eyes.

"No. This isn't the life I want Rob. It never was. I came here today to get an investment for something *I* believe in. I always wanted to leave my own legacy. I don't want to follow in his footsteps. I don't want his future."

"I hear you bro, and I respect it. If you need help with anything, let me know. You know I got you. I'm serious."

The two brothers clasped hands, and Rich walked out of the room feeling refreshed. Not only was he determined to make his business a success, he was determined to prove his father wrong.

Meanwhile during Urban Capital's latest meeting, Marcus knew everything was going as planned, as they had just bought out Jay Foster, but Dezi was on his mind. He couldn't stop thinking about her since he saw her that night.

"She's back," Marcus blurted out during his meeting with Vince and Malik.

"Who?" Vince asked.

"Desirè. She's back home."

"Get the fuck outta here. You serious?" Malik asked.

"Interesting." Vince leaned back in his seat. "So, now what? What does this mean? Will you stay focused?"

"Of course. I'm not interested in making anything serious with her again."

"Lying was never your strong suit. She chose her goals over you. Just keep that in mind," Vince said. "But back to business."

Malik smiled. "See what she talking about though. She might miss that Dreer dick."

"Back to business," Vince repeated.

Marcus cleared his throat "Yea. Back to business."

"Bro, how much capital do we have exactly?" Malik asked Marcus. The two brothers strolled across the Jackson Street bridge looking for lunch.

"More than a nigga can count. A little over eight figures," Marcus said.

"So, we're rich?"

"Not yet, but we will be. Soon."

"The company has eight figures, and we're free to do whatever we want with it. Seems like we rich to me," Malik said.

"Does it feel like it?"

Malik looked at his brother in confusion. "What?"

"Does it feel like we're rich?"

"Eh, not really."

"That's because we're not. That money is accounted for. Every penny of it is reserved to buy D.T. King. Remember that. Until that happens, we won't be rich. Not even close. Nothing has changed in our lifestyles right now."

Malik nodded. "I hear you. You right. Just gotta stay patient I suppose, like you said."

"Remember, it's not about the money. It's about what's ours."

"Ours," Malik cemented.

CHAPTER 5

"There's better ways to die."

RAVEN WAS SO DISAPPOINTED IN the taste of her mimosa. She cringed at the terrible treatment her taste buds had to endure. She quickly signaled for the waitress to come and retrieve it.

"Excuse me, ma'am this is too watered down. Can you bring me another please? Make it strong." Raven gave her a thumbs-up. Once the waitress walked off, she reclined in her chair and checked her phone while the summer breeze tickled her maxi dress. She saw her brother Rich enter the patio dining area. She couldn't contain the smile and joy behind her Celine shades.

"Baby sis, I missed you." Rich gave her petite frame a firm hug and handed her a bouquet of lilies.

Raven blushed. "Aww, for me? You didn't have to."

"It's the least I can do. I know it's been a while since we hung out. How are things?" he asked as he took a seat.

"Everything is going pretty good. You know we all miss you, Rich. You been very distant lately, more so than normal."

"I know, I know, and I apologize for it. I just been grinding and looking for investors for this new project of mine."

"Tell me more," Raven said with enthusiasm as the waitress placed a much stronger mimosa on their table.

Rich handed her prototype photos. "Nubian Noir. It's a lingerie and bikini line for Black women. I've been talking to some people, and it's a good chance I can get a licensing deal."

She looked through the photos in admiration. "Hmm nice. These are sexy. Very different. I know I would wear it. My friends would too since we all have the same style."

"I just need to get the funding, and the rest is history."

"And you will get the funding. I know you will be a major success. I always believed in you."

"Thanks Raven. You really think so?"

"Of course. I wouldn't lie to you. You're different. You have vision. Daddy and Robert have vision also, but they're not like you. You have radical vision. You're striving to create something new."

"Sis, I truly appreciate those words," Rich said as he kissed his younger sister's hand.

After brunch, the siblings went for a walk before they headed back to the parking garage. Rich noticed his sister kept checking her phone.

"You must be expecting an important call or something. You checked your phone like a hundred times," he teased.

Raven attempted to laugh it off. "Just law school crap, that's all. And I haven't heard from my boo all day too."

"I knew it was about a guy. Tell me about him." Rich took his sister's hand and led her across the busy downtown street.

"Well what I *really* like about him is his transparency. He doesn't hold anything in. He's extremely honest. He's such a gentleman. He always opens the door for me. You know, all of the basic chivalrous shit men don't do anymore."

"Hmmm ok. What's his name?"

"Lameer."

"How long y'all been dating?"

"About six months now. I can't wait for you to meet him, Rich. I think he's the one. Like seriously I do."

Rich studied the joy on his sister's face. He had never seen her like this before. He knew the look of true love. It was the same look he had every time he saw Simone. He believed his sister.

"He sounds like a hell of a man. I'm happy for you, and I pray things work out between you two. I'll be meeting him soon enough."

The valet pulled up in Raven's royal Land Rover with Sigma Gamma Rho license plates.

Rich gave her a hug. "It was fun hanging with you today, RaeRae. I'll be in touch."

"Please do, Richie Rich. I miss the family being together."

"I will."

Raven pulled off.

Marcus sat at the table anxiously and constantly checked his watch. *She's not coming*, he thought to himself. And then, she immediately appeared.

Dezi chuckled. "Sorry I'm late. I forgot my sense of direction living in New York all these years."

"No problem. I'm just glad you made it safely."

As the two glanced over the menu, Marcus couldn't help asking the question.

"Why are you back, Dezi? Why now?"

"My mom isn't doing too good, and I just felt it was time to come home."

"I'm sorry to hear that. I hope Mrs. Winters is doing alright. How can I help?"

She replied without hesitation. "Just pray for us. Pray for me." Dezi paused. "Wait. Are you still agnostic these days?"

Marcus chuckled. "I never was agnostic, but I can see how it comes off that way though. I believe in God, but after everything I been through, I just don't trust him."

"What about when God finally gives you what you want?"

"I don't know. The things I wanted passed years ago."

After the server brought their wine, Marcus changed the subject.

"So, tell me more about this nonprofit you've started."

"My partners and I are focused on helping inner city girls obtain college scholarships. Essentially, we plan on giving twenty-five scholarships to seniors in this first year, and we are trying to grow it each year after that. Someone has to give these girls a chance. Many of them don't do anything but sink after high school. They get pregnant if they aren't already, and next thing you know, ten years of their lives have passed. We are hosting a fundraiser next month. I would love if you came."

"I love it. Who are your partners, and how much are you guys trying to raise?"

"We are shooting for twenty-five thousand to start. But hoping for at least ten thousand," Dezi said. "I partnered with my cousin Lauren and an associate of mine I met in New York. He's a good guy."

"I see. Well, I would love to donate. Things are looking better for me these days."

"That'll be great, Marc. Anything would surely be appreciated."

"Plus, it's for a good cause. Would two-hundred-fifty-thousand dollars help?"

Dezi almost choked on her drink. Two-hundred-fifty-thousand dollars? Oh my God. Are you serious, Marcus?"

"So serious. You know I got your back, beautiful. Always have."

"I'm so speechless. I don't know what to say." Dezi felt herself getting moist. She always loved Marcus' spontaneity. He never failed to amaze her.

He laughed. "A thank you would be good for starters. But no seriously, tell your partners y'all have my full support."

Dezi couldn't hide her smile. She stretched out her hand across the table and lightly caressed the top of his hand. She removed it and straightened up her back.

She sipped her wine. "So, what's new with you? Tell me more about this investment firm you started."

"Remember what I told you about years ago? About what my ultimate goal was? Well that's coming sooner than expected."

"Yes, fuck it up bitch!" Simone shouted as ChiChi, her best friend and fellow dancer, twerked on top of the counter. Simone was having a girl's night at the loft, and ChiChi had one too many drinks.

"Post that on my Snap," ChiChi said. She continued to shake her voluptuous ass. Simone had ChiChi's phone and was about to post the video until her phone started to ring.

"Your phone ringing. It's someone name Laro?"

ChiChi immediately stopped dancing and snatched the phone. She hopped off the counter.

"Oh, hell yea. He probably got some money for me," ChiChi said with excitement. Simone picked up her own phone and walked off laughing. One of her other friends began to dance on her, and Simone was smacking her ass with her left hand while she checked her texts with her right hand. The latest text from Rich said: *Another no.*

"Excuse me, boo." Simone got up and headed to the bedroom. Once she was in a semi-quiet area, she called him.

Rich answered on the first ring in a dejected voice.

"Hello."

"Hey, baby what happened?"

"They said no. They won't invest in me." Rich had met with a group of investors in Cleveland that specialized in clothing and retail companies.

"Fuck them! We will find someone to invest. Don't let it get to you, ok? Keep your head up and keep pushing."

"Thanks baby. I could have stayed at home for this shit, but whatever. You're right. I will keep pushing. How is the girl's night?"

"It's going good. All they asses drunk and turnt up as expected. ChiChi somewhere around here making more scam deals."

"That girl is into everything but niggas I see."

"So, what you gonna do for the night?" Simone asked.

"I don't know. Ima find somewhere to get some food and probably just chill at the hotel. Not really feeling adventurous."

"Can't wait 'til you come home tomorrow."

"I'll be there first thing in the morning. Go back and enjoy your party. I'll text you when I'm at the hotel."

"Ok baby, I love you. Have a good night. Remember, don't let this stress you. We will find the money."

"I believe you," Rich replied.

Vince and Malik surveyed the abandoned property, a wide four-story building that had been sitting idle for a few years, maybe more.

"What do you see Malik?" Vince asked.

"A warehouse. Potentially a storage building."

"You don't see money? I see an office building."

Vince took charge of the task of finding a revenue generator for Urban Capital until they assumed control of D.T. King, *if,* they took control. Vince dug into his urban redevelopment plans and decided that a shared office space for small businesses would be the best starting place.

"Something like WeWork or Regus?" Malik asked.

Vince nodded in agreement as the two walked alongside the building. He admired the scene and was finally happy to be living his dream.

"Small business is booming right now. Particularly Black businesses in our communities. Most lack the capital to sign long-term leases for their base of operations. So, we will solve that problem here. We will gut and rehab all four floors. Create over one hundred personal offices for small businesses, including studio space for creative professionals, with a food court in the center. This spot has high visibility. It's a prime location. This will be one of the sparks we need."

"Sounds amazing, fam. You're right about all of that. So, when are we starting?"

"The moment I get a response from this Black nonprofit out of Detroit. They invest in projects like this with business grants. Anything will help, and everything will get rolling."

"This is how you really buy back the block?" Malik asked.

"Yes, it is. Reagan's administration destroyed the Glass-Steagall Act. Black communities got hit the hardest. It's poverty on every corner. Look at all the abandoned homes not too far from here. I heard on the news two homeless men committed suicide yesterday. They were former city workers. There's better ways to die."

Vince shook his head in anger before he continued. "But we will reverse that. We won't need to depend on the city or anyone. We can finance everything ourselves. First, we will establish the business presence, the Black-owned business presence. Then, the homes will follow."

"How long you think it will take to create a new Black Wall Street?"

"Years, decades, maybe even a century. But we will be the ones to start the revolution."

Malik could visualize the aspirations in Vince's head, and he welcomed the opportunity.

Back on his prowl for financing, Rich had been at a networking event for less than an hour and was already annoyed. He had two perspectives on the fraternity of Black entrepreneurs in Chicago:

either they were "wantrapreneurs" who gave off the impression they were big time but really weren't, or they were bougie and turned their nose up at anyone not on their level and refused to share resources.

Rich belonged to neither. Part of what his father said in his office did sting; promoting parties would not generate the wealth he wanted. But he wanted to prove his father wrong. He wanted to beat him, but it was hard to do that when he had no capital.

He retreated to a table and began to pull out his phone and text. Another gentleman sat down as well. Rich noticed him but didn't say anything.

"This is a slow event," the man said.

"Yea, tell me about it."

"I hate these things. I don't even know why I came. Eighty-five percent of the people in here aren't about *real* business anyway."

Rich let out a sigh. "Yea, it's ridiculous. Networking isn't the same these days."

"What I learned about networking is this… it's not about passing out business cards to everyone in the room. It's about establishing a solid relationship with one or two people and building from there."

"That's real, and it makes a lot of sense," Rich said.

The man extended his hand. "What's your name man?"

"I'm Rich."

"Ok cool. Nice to meet you Rich. My name is Marcus Dreer. So, what type of business do you have?"

It was about six o'clock on a Thursday evening. Robert was anxious to get home, as he and his wife Leah were about to embark on a two-week vacation. The email he received from his dad two months ago stalled his getaway just a little while longer.

Robert walked into the main boardroom of D.T. King's headquarters, the war room as they called it. All of the major decisions were made in this room, such as purchasing, selling, or developing property. Large black and white photos of D.T. King's earliest projects lined the wall.

He sat down in the empty room and stared out of the big windows. The weather outside created a cloudy overcast, and a drizzle started to fall. He surveyed the waves in Lake Michigan, leaned back in his chair, and closed his eyes to relax for whatever laid ahead in this supposedly urgent meeting his father called.

Elliot entered the room and interrupted him with his loud voice. "Robert? Didn't expect to see you here."

"A surprise it is." Robert's eyes remained closed. "Did my father message you as well?"

"He did. Said it was important and I had to be here, so here I am." Elliot used animated hand movements. He sat down and attempted to keep the convo going.

"Summer went by fast, didn't it?"

"It's August 3rd. We still have time."

"Where are you and the wife going?"

"Bali. Two weeks." Robert opened his eyes and stared at the wall in front of him. He loathed Elliot.

"Nice! Maybe one day I'll take the wife there."

"It would have been a great honeymoon spot for you."

"I can't afford a two-week vacation in Bali, Robert. I don't have long money like you." Elliot's voice revealed a hint of sarcasm. "It'll be a nice Christmas gift though. Put it on your list."

"I'll give you a bottle of Scotch. How about that?"

"No thank you. I don't drink. And in my family, it's considered an insult to the birth of Jesus to even think about alcohol around that time."

"Ok."

"But the trip to Bali would suffice. Or you can loan me the money and I'll pay you back."

Robert checked his watch in irritation. "Elliot, aren't you from Dallas?"

"Yessir."

"Your family owned a small chain of ice cream shops. I'm sure that helped put you through school, right?"

"Something like that. What's your point here?"

"I'm not the only one who comes from money."

"Did you work for your money Robert, or was it handed to you?" Elliot shot back.

"Don't ever ask me about hard work." Robert shifted his body to face Elliot head on across the table. "I wouldn't be where I am now if it wasn't for hard work."

Elliot knew a thing or two about hard work himself. He came from a devout religious family that believed the Bible and business were intertwined. Yes, it was true his parents opened an ice cream parlor when he was eleven years old. His parents put every penny they had into it.

One day, his parents were in a bad car accident. His mother thankfully walked away with minor injuries, but it left his father, a Deacon at their church, paralyzed from the waist down. Elliot stepped up to help his mother with the day-to-day operations the best he could. His business sense was immaculate at an early age. The ice cream parlor became so successful, they opened a second location when he was in high school. Elliot didn't own a car, so he walked to school with his younger sister every day. He would then ensure she had money to take the bus home while he walked to the parlor after school to work. He became the manager of the second location while his mom managed the original, and his father ran the books from home.

His parents eventually became burned out. Some businessmen based out of Fort Worth caught wind of their success and made them an offer to buy them out and expand. The Briggs sold their business for roughly three million and a half dollars. Although he understood his parents' decision, he wished they didn't sell. He wanted to grow the family business organically. Elliot attended a community college to work and save up more money for college.

He didn't want his parents to use all of their money on his education because it was all they had. His parents respected his wishes and promised to cover whatever he couldn't pay. Elliot accepted the offer and eventually enrolled into Oklahoma State University. After graduation, he landed a job offer in Chicago at a bank and soon became bored. Once he saw a job listing for the position of a project manager at the D. T. King firm, he jumped on it. The rest was history. He rose up the ranks due to his exceptional business sense and ultimately became Senior Vice President. He loved his career and he loved working for D.T. King. Elliot loved hard work.

Roland entered the room. "Gentlemen, thank you for meeting with me. Sorry about my tardiness."

Robert and Elliot both changed their demeanor as the CEO sat down at the head of the table and folded his hands. Roland looked at Robert and then Elliot.

"As you both know, I plan on stepping down from my CEO position a little over a year from now to just focus on running the board. It's been a long journey, but I feel it's time for me to pass the torch. With that being said, I felt it would be a perfect time to address this. There is a strong belief that you, Robert, will take my role automatically as the next CEO. This is a family business after all. But Elliot, I consider you family as well. You're like another son to me."

Robert started feeling uneasy as his posture shifted.

"So, from this moment on," Roland continued, "the two of you will be evaluated *heavily* to see who my successor will be."

Roland's statement generated contrasting moods. Elliot grinned, feeling honored and ecstatic about the news, while Robert felt stunned and demoralized. He kept his poker face on.

Roland stood up before delivering his final statement. "There are no handouts here gentlemen. This company is my baby, and everything must be earned. Never forget that." He strolled out the room.

Elliot turned to Robert and extended his hand with a smile. "Well, this will be fun. May the best man win."

Robert sat there speechless and stared at his newly declared rival as he fumed with anger, betrayal, and disappointment.

Marcus noticed Vince's look of frustration when he walked into the office.

Vince got straight to the point. "We've got a small problem."

"What's the issue?"

"Marid Jabbar refuses to sell to us." Marid was one of the top shareholders in D.T. King—an Afro-Iranian businessman and principal owner of several companies, all holding firms for franchises, mainly fast food places. His share in D.T. King was side money, and his net worth was just as big as Roland Thompson.

"What's he saying?"

"He just declined twice."

"I'll talk to him."

"And what are you going to say? Please sell us your shares?" Vince asked.

"I just want to pick his brain. That's all."

"Let me know how that works."

Marcus retreated to his private office and texted Dezi.

"You should come by later on. I'll make you dinner."

She instantly responded with *okay* and included the heart eye emoji. Marcus wanted Dezi back as his woman, and he was going all out.

CHAPTER 6
"That has a ring to it..."

VINCE PACKED HIS SUITCASE METHODICALLY and precisely.

Janelle strolled into the bedroom and placed her arms around him from behind.

"How long will you be away for?"

Vince continued to pack. "Just the weekend. Three days. There is a big real estate conference in Detroit. I'm the best suited to attend for the company."

Janelle sat down on the edge of the bed. "I still can't believe you left WestGate for this."

"For what?" Vince stopped packing. "That place didn't care about me, and I didn't care about them. I'm making nearly thirty-grand more now."

Janelle's lips formed a pout. "I don't know. Yeah you make more money now, but I just never took Marcus serious when it came to these things. And now he convinced you to quit your job and you're working more hours. The kids miss you, Vince."

Vince resumed packing. "Janelle, I need you to understand that what I'm doing is real. It's not just for me. It's for you and those kids. I haven't felt this alive in years when it came to work. Marcus and I had these dreams since we were little. You know that. Once the business gets settled, I will go back to working normal hours. I promise."

"Have you thought about what I said?" Janelle asked.

"We aren't getting a new house."

"Why not? We're outgrowing this place, Vince. The kids are getting bigger and they need their space. You just said you're making more money, so what's the issue?"

"I'm very aware of that, but do you have the money to contribute to that? Or am I expected to figure all of this out on my own?"

"You know I don't make enough money for all of that."

"But I'm swimming in money, huh? It's nothing wrong with this house at all. Is this even about the kids? Or is this about you?"

Janelle got quiet. "Ok." She walked out of the room.

Vince stood there and massaged his temples. He purchased their bungalow home in the South suburbs of Chicago as a steal right after the housing crisis in 2008. He had just graduated from grad school and made the responsible decision to purchase a home for his growing family. Yes, the house was small, but it was in good shape. Vince made sure of it. There was no true need for them to move. He just felt Janelle was using those excuses as a reason to force him to do things her way, which she had done for so many years, and he was tired of it. He wasn't going to let her control *his* life anymore. He made the executive decision.

The angel investor Rich had been searching high and low for had finally come. Marcus Dreer had invested the full one-point-three million Rich needed to start his business, Nubian Noir. Their official meeting went perfect and the full investment, in the form of cash, was in his possession. Now Rich, armed with Marcus' money, was finally able to execute.

Simone couldn't hide her excitement either as Rich navigated the car through the Chicago traffic.

"Yaasss baby! I'm so damn happy for you. I want to be a part of it every step of the way."

"Trust and believe you will be. You're going to be the main model for the line as soon as we get this first shipment done."

"No," Simone objected. "I wanna be more than the model. I want to be involved with this, Rich. I believe in you, and I believe in this business."

"You *will* be involved I promise you that. What do you wanna be?"

"I want to work in marketing, not just showcasing my body. I want to be a part of the creative decisions."

"Done," Rich replied as he smothered her with kisses at a red light.

Malik pulled up to Marcus' house in his new 2017 cherry red Jaguar Sedan.

Marcus looked puzzled as he walked outside. "What is this?"

"It's mine, that's what it is."

"No shit. What I mean is, how did you get this?"

"When your credit score is 780 and you work hard all summer, you play harder bro. Just something I came up on with the remaining of my savings."

"You're a good saver," Marcus said. "Well shit. Let's go around the corner and see how it ride."

Malik turned up Chance's "No Problems" song. "Hop in then."

Marcus felt his brother was lying deep down in his heart. Something was up with Malik, and he was going to find out.

Vince carried himself with the utmost confidence surrounded by fellow real estate professionals in the hotel lobby after day one of the conference concluded. Vince wasn't a real estate professional per se. He was still learning the game. His background was finance and management, so he *knew* how money worked. Nevertheless, everyone around him was deep into the game of real estate. He was just a rookie, but he wasn't going to let them know that.

Vince settled into a lounge and engaged in a social conversation with a group of younger executives. One of them caught his eye. Her mahogany complexion and fierce cheekbones commanded his attention. Her size eight frame fit snugly in her violet dress. After a while many people dispersed, leaving Vince and the woman alone in the lobby.

"I'm sorry, how do you pronounce your name? Is it Ad-jew-ah?" Vince asked.

"Bingo. If I got a deposit for every time someone mispronounced it, I'll be a little bit richer. Your name is Vince, correct?" Adjoa asked.

"That's right. You're good with names I see."

"I try to be. My father always told me there's power in names, so never forget them. Tell me more about your business."

Vince sat back and loosened his tie. "Well, it's Urban Capital. We're a holding company that invests in real estate-oriented ventures. My best friend is the founder, but he recruited me and made me a partner in the company. I'm here trying to make some strong connections for us as we move forward."

"That's amazing to hear. And you guys are based out of Chicago?" Adjoa asked.

"Yep. What about yourself?"

"I'm out of New Jersey. My parents moved here from Ghana years ago and were fortunate enough to buy their first property just before I was born. Now here I am years later keeping the family tradition strong."

"Is it just you now? Running the business?"

"Yes, it's just me. My father passed away a few years ago."

"I'm sorry to hear that. How old are you?" Vince asked.

"No worries. Thank you. I'm forty-one."

"Stop lying." Vince was taken aback. She looked his age but was nine years his senior.

She blushed. "Don't try to butter me up. So, what did you take away from this first day?"

Vince exhaled. "There was so much wealth of knowledge. I don't know where to start."

"I learned that it's imperative to stay the course no matter how rocky things may get. In this field people get nervous so fast and want to hop to the next thing instead of being patient."

"Would you say patience is necessary in all things?"

"Of course. The issue is everyone is just in a big damn hurry all the time. If we slow down and don't rush things, everyone would be in better positions."

Vince smiled. "You're preaching to the choir right now."

Adjoa changed subjects. "Are you staying in this hotel?"

"No, actually I'm not. I'm across the street in the other one."

"Oh, ok. I never stay in the host hotels either. Well, I'll be keeping in touch with you, and I hope to see you again this weekend." Adjoa gathered her things and prepared to leave.

Vince fixated his eyes on her. "Most definitely."

"What was your last name again?" Adjoa asked before she walked off.

"Brown."

"Vince Brown. It has a ring to it, Mr. Brown."

Adjoa seduced him with her eyes as she strutted off. Vince felt a rush of lust, but even greater, he felt a craving he had to satisfy.

Marcus walked into the worn office building that served as the headquarters for Marid Jabbar's business ventures. He heard Marid was horrible with time and could be loud and annoying. Marid greeted him.

"Ah yes, Marcus!" he said in his strong accent. "Come into my office."

His office was cluttered with papers, books, numerous versions of the Quran, and a bunch of miscellaneous things, such as vacuum cleaners and old desktop computers from the nineties. The place was a wreck. A large flag of Iran hung on the wall behind his desk.

Marcus sat down and got straight to business. "Marid, I'm here to purchase your shares in D.T. King. I wanna buy you out."

Marid chuckled. "No." He shoved a donut into his mouth, and the crumbs fell into the clutches of his beard. "I have no intentions to sell unless it is capital gain. You don't have enough money to buy me out."

"Well, I was thinking perhaps we can come to an agreement. That's why I'm here."

"Look, you are cheap okay. You're not an elite business man like myself and my partners. Roland Thompson has made me a lot of money lately. I intend to keep it that way."

"You haven't even heard my offer."

"Doesn't matter what the offer is. I don't plan to sell, and you don't have enough money."

"Well, I strongly hope you would reconsider. We will meet again." Marcus stood up and exited the office slightly frustrated.

"Earnings are up roughly three-point seven percent from this time last year. If we continue to play it safe, we could scale another one percent by February," Robert told the committee as he lectured them on D.T. King's land leasing division.

Elliot interrupted him. "Actually, based on my calculations we can scale up by at least three percent max. Why play it safe when we have nothing to lose?"

"Because in this business anything can happen. Look at the Indianapolis project. It's a disaster."

"A disaster that you signed off on," Elliot said. The others in the room felt the tension rising.

Robert masked his anger. "The Indianapolis project is a project we all look at in hindsight as one of our less favorable decisions." Out of Robert's peripheral vision he saw his father peek into the room. Robert broke into a sweat.

He stared down Elliot with fury. "Now shall I continue?"

The last day of the conference wore Vince out. He laid on his bed staring up at the ceiling. He was tired but confident with the connections he made over the weekend. He got up to pour himself a drink but realized he had no ice. He headed down the hallway to the ice machine in his white beater and slacks. He saw Adjoa coming off the elevator.

"Hey. Your room is on this floor too?" he asked.

She smiled at him. "Hi Mr. Brown. No, I'm just making my rounds. It's a habit whenever I visit one of my hotels."

Vince was confused. "One of your hotels?"

"Yes. I'm sorry, I thought I told you. I own this hotel. I own seven."

Vince cocked his head at her and laughed. "Wow. You sure do know how to keep a secret don't you. You're amazing."

"Have you enjoyed your stay here this weekend?"

"I most certainly have."

"Well I'm happy to hear that." She grazed his left bicep. "Well, I won't disturb you. I'll carry on." She began to walk down the hallway.

"Hey. You want to step in my room? Have a chat and a drink? No need to do your rounds. I'm sure everything is fine."

Adjoa stopped immediately in her tracks and turned around. "That sounds like a plan to me." She was hoping he would invite her, and simultaneously, he hoped she would oblige.

CHAPTER 7

"...YOU SURE ABOUT THIS?"

RICH'S PERSEVERANCE PAID OFF. HE wasted no time building his infrastructure. He hired all of the necessary staff and rented an office space in Chicago's West Loop. He had never been as happy as he was now. It was a dream come true, and his prayers were answered. Rich Thompson was determined to prove his father wrong.

"Tell me what your vision is?" Rich asked Angelo Simmons, his newly hired Director of Operations. Angelo was a plump dark-skinned, well-dressed man. He was gay, but his sexual preference didn't bother Rich at all. He knew Angelo would be the best man for the job.

"Women don't just wanna look good for men. They wanna look good for themselves," Angelo explained in his soft smooth voice. Angelo knew business. He was formerly a district manager for a major retail chain but became frustrated with the company after a series of questionable racist ads. He saw the job posting for Rich's company and jumped on it.

"We need to focus on things from a woman's perspective, not ours. I want to organize a series of surveys and focus groups from the demographics of eighteen to twenty-two, twenty-three to thirty, and thirty-one to forty."

"You seem to know your shit, Mr. Simmons."

"This isn't my first rodeo."

"How was Detroit?" Malik asked as his teeth sliced through a moist brownie. The team met to discuss potential investments that could keep their cash flow coming in outside of the D.T. King acquisition, *if* they weren't able to acquire it.

"It was real nice. Very nice. I networked with a lot of people that can benefit us in the future," Vince replied.

"Good. I knew you would be able to hold your own there," Marcus said. "That's why I knew it would be best for you to go."

The conference room phone suddenly rang, interrupting their meeting.

Marcus pressed the answer button. "Hello?"

"Hi Marcus? This is David Stevenson over at CityTrust Bank. How are ya?"

"Pretty good. What about you?"

"Doing alright." David paused for a second. "So um, that property that you guys had your sight on is off the market. It's been sold. We had a buyer this morning."

Everyone's body language in the room changed. Malik looked at Vince and then back at his brother. Vince leaned forward with a disappointed look on his face. Marcus just stared at the phone.

"Who bought it?" Marcus asked.

"A guy name Mr. Jabbar. He paid cash."

Marcus and Vince made eye contact. *This son of bitch!* Marcus thought to himself.

"Ok, thanks for the update David. We will call you back." Marcus ended the call.

"Damn, how the fuck this happen? What we gonna do now?" Malik asked.

"There are more properties out there. We just have to keep searching." Vince sounded optimistic.

"No, fuck that! This dude refuses to sell us his shares in D.T. King, and then he buys a property no one cared about until now? It's an insult. We *will* get what's ours," Marcus said.

"How? He's not going to sell that building to us," Vince said.

"Yea I know, but where there is a will, there is a way."

Malik finished typing a text. "What you got in mind, bro?"

"If he don't want to move out the way, we will push him out the way. Ima figure something out."

Dezi waited for Marcus in the lobby of the community arts center in the Woodlawn neighborhood. Marcus rushed through the door as if he was late for an interview.

"Sorry for keeping you waiting." Marcus kissed her on the cheek.

"No worries at all. You must've had a busy day today."

"Busy is an understatement. Got some issues with this property we were trying to buy amongst other things." He paused to study her body, her curvy physique. Marcus *loved* everything about Dezi and would do *anything* for her.

The feeling was mutual.

Dezi loved Marcus. She just hated to be in his shadow, which was why she left him years ago and decided to relocate to New York. Nevertheless, she loved him. She never met anyone who was as ambitious as him. It turned her on to a level she couldn't describe. The way he looked in his blue suit mesmerized her and made her weak. She did a great job of concealing it though.

"Marcus, you sure about this?"

"Yes, I'm sure. You're doing this for a great cause, so it's a no-brainer for me to support."

Dezi was ready to introduce him to the board of directors of her non-profit organization to make his generous donation formal. The first person was Dezi's cousin, Lauren. Marcus remembered her from back in the day as the two embraced. He didn't know the man, but his name rang a bell. Dion Lewis was the new weekend weatherman for ABC 7, the Chicago news affiliate.

"So, you're Marcus. It's a pleasure to meet you. Dezi has raved about you a lot. We truly appreciate your donation," Dion said.

"Thank you. It's no problem at all. I support my people," Marcus said. The four began to discuss the plans of the organization. Dezi and Marcus were in sync the entire time, not physically but emotionally.

Lauren left immediately after the meeting. Dion prepared to leave not long after. He kissed Dezi on her cheek and told her he'd see her later.

"Are you two dating or something?" Marcus asked.

"What makes you say that?"

"I don't know. Body language I guess."

"Me and him are complicated. Let's just say that."

"Oh, ok. I understand."

"Marcus…" Dezi walked over to him and placed her hand on his cheek. "I missed you. Thank you for this."

"I already told you it's no problem." Marcus rested his right hand on her hip. "I missed you more though."

Dezi kissed him with a fury of passion. Marcus tightened his grip on her waist, securing what always belonged to him. Dezi stopped and looked deep into his eyes.

"I want it. Fuck me how you always do. Please…" she begged.

Marcus said no words. He obliged her request and grabbed her left arm as he walked over to the desk. He bent her over until she had a full coke bottle arch and aggressively raised her dress. He pulled down her panties in one full motion. Her pussy was already a wet mess, her juices dripped down the side of her thighs. He pulled his pants down. His penis was at full attention, ready for the kill. He gripped both of her ass cheeks and slid into her, deeply and slowly. Then, he began to give fast and powerful strokes.

Dezi's mouth was wide open as she felt Marcus going to work on her. She gripped the edge of the desk to brace herself, loving every bit of it. She had been missing this for a long time. She needed it.

Marcus left the arts center feeling like a new man, a focused man. He was hungry after that midday workout, so he stopped at Lil Carl's and ordered a large gizzard and wing combo. He was determined to figure out a way to take down Marid Jabbar. Yes, he was pissed that Marid bought the building Urban Capital was about to acquire, but he really wanted Marid's shares in D.T. King to get closer to Roland Thompson.

"Alright, you boys are good to go," Carl told two teenage customers.

"Aye can we get two cookies?" one of the boys asked.

"What flavor? Chocolate chip, oatmeal raisin, or butter?"

The two boys laughed. "Nah old man, not real cookies. Loose squares." The boy stuck an imaginary cigarette in his mouth.

"What?" Carl asked. "Na, I ain't got no loose squares. This here is a food establishment."

"My bad, we ain't on bullshit with you," the other boy said. "John Sharks over on 147th sell 'em, so we just figured y'all did too." The teenagers exited the store.

Marcus swallowed a mouthful of gizzards and fries. "A chicken joint selling tobacco? What the hell has the world come to?"

Carl shook his head and went to work on phone orders. "Them mothafuckas will sell anything for a profit."

Marcus sat back and pulled out his phone and googled the owners of the John Sharks restaurant on 147th street. The business was franchised by a private company named Chicagoland Food Investments LLC. He searched the company name on the Illinois Secretary of State website. He had hit the lottery. The registered agent for this company was none other than Marid Jabbar.

"I think I figured out who our cookie monster is, Carl," Marcus said in a devious voice.

A few hours later Marcus was parked in the lot of John Sharks deep in thought when EC stepped into the car from the passenger side. The two looked at each other and EC, without saying a word, showed him a baggie with two cigarettes.

Another lash from the whip slammed against Robert's flesh. His Dom, his wife Leah, was punishing him.

"I need you to be a good boy if you want your dick in my mouth. Do you understand me?" Leah demanded.

Robert exhaled in pleasure. "Yes, Madam Thompson."

"Good boy." She gave him another whip before she got on her knees.

Robert and his family lived in a lavish contemporary brickstone in the Wicker Park neighborhood just north of downtown. Their kids weren't home at the moment, so the couple indulged in their BDSM fantasy. Although Robert *loved* to be dominated by Leah, this time she sensed something was seriously wrong with her husband. After their sexual fantasy concluded, she tried to console him.

"What's wrong baby?"

"I just don't get it," Robert blurted out. "I'm his fucking son. I give my all to this company. I've done that my entire life, and he insults me by considering this church boy over me."

Leah began to massage Robert's shoulders. "Elliot isn't half the business man you are, and he isn't a Thompson."

"Then why the hell is he even being considered?"

"You know why. Cause your father is an asshole. He doesn't care about family, he cares about himself. He doesn't think you are worthy Robert."

Robert sulked at her response, although he already knew this deep down inside.

"But he is wrong, and he will see. He can keep up this silly ass competition all he wants, but you will prevail regardless."

"Thank you, baby. I'm going to take the fight to Elliot from now on. I will control the game," Robert said.

Raven couldn't focus on the pile of books scattered in front of her. The fall semester just started a few weeks ago, but the strain of law school had already taken its toll. She had been in the library for about three hours on this cool September evening. She began to do some online shopping to refresh her mind when her phone buzzed. It was a text message from Lameer.

How's studying coming along?

Draining. I need you to hold me.

I'll be over there tonight, and you can have whatever you want.

She couldn't contain her smile as she read his response. That text sent a rush directly to the oasis between her thighs. She replied with the kissing face emoji.

Can't wait. So when you gonna stop running and meet my fam bae? They really want to see you.

Lameer didn't respond until an hour later.

On my way boo. And don't worry I'll be meeting your family soon. Very soon. Raven sat in the midst of traffic as she headed home to her condo. She pulled out her phone and replied.

Okay.

Marcus walked in Marid's office with one objective in mind, a simple business proposition.

"Oh Marcus, you back again I see. You must like me," Marid said.

Marcus just stood there, declining to sit down. "How much are you willing to sell your shares in D.T. King for?"

Marid laughed. "I told your silly ass already. I'm not for sale. You don't buy me out, everything I do buys you out. You should know that by now. That was a very nice property. I can't wait to sell it for double."

Marcus pulled out a tablet and brought up a MOV file on the screen. He pressed play. The footage was from a body cam of multiple people purchasing illegal cigarettes from Marid's various John Sharks restaurants in the area. The footage contained the keyword "cookies" to tip off employees that they wanted to buy cigarettes. It also included the John Sharks logo along with dates, time stamps, and lastly, a screenshot of Marid Jabbar as the registered owner.

Marid stared down Marcus as he rose from his seat in shock.

"Do you want to do business? Or do you want to be stupid?" Marcus finally sat down and crossed his legs. "What I have here is enough evidence to send to the State's Attorney's office. Your stores will be shut down immediately, and you will be prosecuted. You will lose everything—your precious LLC, your nasty ass chicken restaurants, all of that shit."

Marcus put the tablet away. "But it doesn't have to be like this Marid. It really doesn't. You can keep all of it. Everything. I don't care about your damn restaurants. I just want your shares in D.T. King. Sell them *all* to me now. Below market value, and all of this can end today."

Marcus showed Marid how far he would go to get what he wanted. Marid knew he had been breached. "You can have the damn shares. Just don't leak this footage. These businesses are all I have."

"I don't want to hear shit from you ever again. One false move and I promise you I will ruin you. And one last thing. That building you bought? That belongs to us too. You will transfer over the deed ASAP for my generosity of course."

Marid Jabbar was speechless and defeated. After that final blow, Marcus towered over his enemy and stared at him with rage. And then he walked out.

CHAPTER 8
"ONLY BY BLOOD..."

RICH PRACTICALLY LIVED IN THE office now, as he went over numbers constantly, fervently, making sure there were no mistakes. Time had moved fast, and the November sky faded into darkness. He had meetings to attend, people to see, moves to make. He was determined. He knew he could be successful, and he wouldn't stop until he was.

Simone walked up and sat down next to him. She placed her hand on his right leg.

"Isn't that enough work for one day, baby?"

"It's never enough." Rich remained focus on the projections in front of him. "Shouldn't *you* be getting ready for work? It's almost ten p.m."

"I'm not going in tonight."

Rich stopped what he was doing and looked at her. "Why not?"

"I want to be with you. This is where my heart is now. I never cared for dancing. It just blew up."

Simone Hale, also known as FrenchKiss on the stage, was only twenty-four years old. She grew up in the Chicago South suburb Dolton. Her athletic build matured faster than many girls in her age group. Of course, she caught the attention of many men, young and old. She was eventually recruited by independent music producer Mike Capone, who used her as a model in his various music videos. She began to make decent money for a teenage girl.

She tried to get her education on the right track by attending general courses at a community college where she developed a keen interest in marketing. She loved learning everything about the science behind luring a person into buying a product or service. Making them *believe* they needed it.

When she was out with her friends one night, they went to a strip club. It was amateur night. Her friends urged her to go up on stage since she had an amazing body and twerking skills. She obliged, and the crowd was in awe. The manager noticed her skills and asked if she was interested in doing this part time. Eventually, she agreed to be a part-time dancer, and it wasn't long before her talents and beauty made her the main attraction.

She began working at The Pyramid, the most prestigious gentlemen's club on Chicago's South Side. It was there she met Rich Thompson. Rich was in love with her from the moment he met her. After his private dance, Rich just held and embraced her. Their souls meshed. Something in her spirit convinced her it wasn't fake, it was real. Both of them were broken and needed each other, and that's why their paths crossed that night in a private room of a strip club. Simone had never *ever* performed a sexual act on anyone in a club, but that night, she and Rich made love in the private room, and they've been together ever since.

She loved everything about him—his ambition, his caring nature. She had never loved a man a day in her life. After she met Rich, her enthusiasm for dancing slowly diminished, and her passion for marketing was re-born. She never believed she could do it, but now that Rich had started a business with lots of potential, she wanted to be a part of that. She wanted to live out their dreams together.

"What are we doing for Thanksgiving? I'm not really feeling it this year. Don't care to have a get together at the crib again," Rich said. Every year the couple hosted holiday parties at his loft, but this year Rich wanted to tone it down.

"We can have it at my place," Simone suggested.

Rich chuckled. "You haven't been there in months. You sure it's not a ghost living there now?"

Simone laughed. "I want to sell it, but no one is buying these days."

"I hear you, but honestly, I just don't want that type of crowd this year period. I want it to be simple. Maybe we can go to my parent's house."

Simone proceeded with caution. "But after that last meeting with your father, I thought you was done with them?"

"Done with him, yes. But not the rest of my family. Plus, my sister and mom have been dying to meet you. This can be a perfect opportunity."

"Ok baby, if that's what you want, that's what it will be." Simone kissed her man.

Rich really didn't care about her meeting his family. He was fine with how things were now. He just wanted to prove his father wrong to his face and show him he was doing well without him.

"Vanessa share with your brother."

Vince instructed his seven-year-old daughter to pass her younger sibling the iPad. Vince and Janelle had three beautiful children. His baby boy Victor was four. He was a sweet little boy that inherited his father's kind side. Vanessa had his fiery business acumen. Janice was the oldest child of their union. She was fourteen. Janelle and Vince were only juniors in high school when she was born. Janice looked every bit like Janelle and acted like her too. She had her attitude and everything. She was now at that stage in life when family annoyed her, and she only wanted to be with her friends and boys.

Vince was enjoying his time with the two younger kids watching

Netflix in the entertainment room. Janelle walked in seemingly frustrated.

"Can you come here for a minute," she asked her husband. Vince, sensing the incoming bullshit, reluctantly got up and followed her into the kitchen.

"What is it?" he asked.

"I want to take a family trip."

"Ok, when? Where?"

"I don't care. Soon though. You don't spend enough time with us."

Vince raised his voice slightly. "What the hell are you talking about woman? Whenever I'm not working, I'm here."

"That's the damn problem Vincent, you're *always* working. You work more than you ever did before."

"I'm working to make a better life for them kids and your greedy ass," Vince shouted. Vanessa and Victor took notice in the other room. "I've been working all of my life to support you. My entire life. Everything we have is because of me. How dare you say that?"

"That's what you're supposed to do nigga. Don't give me that sob story. The fact is you're still not present in our lives as much as you need to be."

"I'm not about to deal with this shit tonight."

Vince stormed off. He put on his shoes and coat and walked out the door as Janelle cut her eyes at him.

Vince got in his car and pulled off. "Don't Say Goodnight" by the Isley Brothers filled his car as he cruised through the residential streets. He reached behind his driver seat and grabbed a half full bottle of Remy XO that was chilled from the fall elements. He took a strong swig from it, and then he went through his contacts on his Bluetooth and pressed the call button. Adjoa's calming voice answered after a few rings.

"Hello."

"Hey lovely, how are you? Is this a good time?" Vince asked.

"Yes, it is. I'm doing well, and yourself? I'm happy to hear from you."

"I'm doing ok, I guess. Just needed someone to talk to."

"Talk to me, Mr. Brown," Adjoa instructed him. Vince had grown closer to her ever since their sexual encounter back in July, and she was the perfect remedy to his misery infected marriage.

The Dreer brothers were relaxing at Marcus' home watching the Bulls game and drinking.

"Where's the foul?" Malik shouted at the TV as he grabbed another beer.

"These fools trying to blow the game," Marcus said.

"So, what's the plans for Thanksgiving?"

"Ima go to Dezi's family house. What about you?"

"That's crazy she back now out of nowhere and y'all ain't missed a beat, huh?"

"It is crazy, but I ain't complaining at all. Just living in the moment with it."

"Well, I'm going to probably stop by Aunt Deborah's place."

"I see."

"They been asking about you a lot lately," Malik said.

"For what?"

"Just to see how you been and how the business is going."

"They don't give a fuck about that," Marcus said.

"Marc...they need some help man, for real. They about to be evicted at the end of the month."

"Not our problem."

"Bro...come on man, we got the money to help them. We have to. They're our family."

"Only by blood." Marcus was fed up with the conversation. "They *never* gave a helping hand out of all the shit we been through.

Where were they when mom was sick? Where were they when we was down to our last dime? Fuck them! They didn't come around before, so don't come around now. Debbie probably throw away all her money gambling. They're all stupid and can't budget for shit. I have no sympathy for them."

"Iight man."

Marcus continued his rant. "The only family I consider, the only family I care about is you, Vince, and lowkey Dezi. No one else matters to me. That's what I care about more than anything. My *real* family."

"Ok. I respect that bro. I hear you." Malik stood up and went to the kitchen.

Marcus sat there and felt his blood boiling as he downed a beer. The audacity of his fucking 'family.' They never cared about him and his brother. His thoughts grew more and more hostile.

"Iight bro, I'm 'bout to head back home before this storm hit." Malik re-emerged from the kitchen and clasped hands with Marcus.

"Bet. Be safe out there and let me know when you make it home."

Marcus closed the door behind him. He sunk himself into his love seat and text Dezi.

What all do you need me to bring for Thanksgiving? Your sister still love peach cobbler with no peaches? Lol.

Twenty minutes passed before Dezi replied.

Hey boo. About Thanksgiving... maybe it'll be best if you didn't come. It's a lot going on and I just don't want to include you in this right now. I'll explain more later. I hope you understand. Love you.

That text hit Marcus in the chest. He looked forward to being with the woman he loved for the holiday and being around her family. After all, her family always did like him. He didn't know what the issue was, but he was disappointed.

He just replied with a simple, *ok no worries*, and then set his phone down. Marcus cracked open another beer while watching the Bulls lose their lead in the fourth quarter.

Today wasn't his day.

"Yaass bro! Yasssss!" Raven screamed as Rich showed her his office and explained all of the recent transactions his company made. His products were now in select stores on the West coast and Southeast. He felt good.

"Thank you, sis. Thank you so much," Rich said.

Raven inspected a mannequin sporting a red bikini. "When can I model some of these? This is fucking cute, oh my god!"

"Um never. You aren't modeling anything." Rich's big brother persona came out.

"Why not? I'm grown. Y'all gotta stop acting like I'm still a kid."

"I'll be coming to Thanksgiving," Rich said, changing the subject.

Her face lit up again. "Really? Wow, this is a first in I don't know how many years."

"Yep, I told mama yesterday. I'm bringing Simone as well."

"Great. I look forward to meeting and getting to know her."

"Why you so thirsty to meet her?"

Raven shrugged. "I feel like you been hiding her all this time, but I feel like you been hiding yourself also so..."

Rich didn't consider it hiding. He just felt comfortable not coming around his family. His father's overbearing personality and his brother's kiss-ass mentality was just too annoying for him. Rich wanted to make a statement this year, and he looked forward to it.

CHAPTER 9

"THINGS WILL NEVER BE THE SAME."

SIMONE'S NERVOUSNESS SHOWED AS SHE constantly fidgeted with her luxury purse.

"You ok?" Rich asked.

"Yea, I'm cool. You sure this dress is ok? It ain't too revealing? I shoulda wore something else."

"Baby yes, you look perfect. You asked that like five times. Everything will be okay. Trust me"

"Ok." She intertwined her left hand with his right, as the two turned onto the block of the Thompson house.

"There it is," Rich said as they approached the house. "Home."

Simone looked astonished. "Damn."

The Thompson estate was located deep in the heart of the Beverly neighborhood. The massive home sat on a gentle hill surrounded by trees. The autumn leaves were sprinkled all over the picture-perfect lawn. The English style exterior replicated a castle fit for royalty. Rich backed his Audi into the driveway. He and Simone got out in unison.

Simone clung to his side as they walked toward the home. "This driveway is long as hell. It's like a street by itself."

"Tell me about. Imagine having to shovel this thing."

Simone laughed. "Your parents made you shovel this? Why y'all ain't hire nobody?"

"My father didn't want us growing up feeling entitled, so my brother and I were in charge of all the landscape and yard work duties. We had to work early on."

The driveway was packed with cars, which suggested that everyone had already arrived. He saw his brother's Yukon Denali and Raven's Land Rover. The two moved past the four-car garage and ascended up the stairs. Within two seconds of ringing the bell, the door flew open.

"Well hello!" Leah said with excitement. "I'm glad you made it, bro."

"Better late than never, right?"

"Come here and gimme a hug. It's been a long time." The two embraced.

"This is my girlfriend, Simone. Simone, this is my sister-in-law, Leah."

"Hi, nice to meet you." Simone extended her hand. Leah ignored her gesture and gave her a hug instead.

"Nice to meet you. Thank you for coming. I love that dress. It's cute! Do you run track? Your body is so toned." Leah showered her with compliments.

Simone blushed slightly. "No, I don't play sports, but thank you so much."

The house was consumed with noise from television and constant chatter. Leah took their coats and hung them up as Rich's seven-year old nephew RJ and his five-year old niece Regina ambushed him.

"Uncle Richie!" they screamed in unison as they smothered him with hugs.

"How y'all been? Uncle Rich miss y'all." While Rich entertained the young kids, Simone surveyed the marble flooring and massive chandelier that hung from the ceiling.

"It was imported from Italy." Rich interrupted her gaze.

"It's beautiful."

"Yes, it is. Come on, let's make our rounds."

"Well, look what the wind blew in." Robert appeared from the kitchen. "And you must be Simone. It's a pleasure to finally meet my future sister-in-law."

Simone flashed a wide grin. "Nice to meet you."

"Excuse our tardiness," Rich said.

"Don't worry about that. We're just glad you're here. You don't understand how much this means."

The three walked in the living room area where majority of the family lounged around. Roland sat in a plush recliner holding a glass of scotch.

"You made it," Roland said with a rare smile. Rich took his greeting as hollow words, a show for the audience. Roland walked toward them and gave Rich a pat on the back and then hugged Simone. "And what's your name, sweetie?"

"It's Simone dad," Raven interjected before Simone had the chance to answer. "Hey boo." Raven welcomed Simone with warmness.

"Go on in there and speak to your mother and aunts. The food should be ready shortly. Raven give, uh, Simone here a tour of the house."

"I've been waiting to meet you for so long. Come on, follow me. You want some wine or champagne?" Raven asked.

"Wine would be nice." Simone let Raven lead the way.

Rich walked into the massive open kitchen as his mother Gloria and her sisters slaved away cooking dinner.

"Hey mama."

"Baby! You made it. I'm so glad you're here. Where is that woman of yours?" she asked.

"Raven is giving her a quick tour of the house."

"Well, y'all got here just in time. Dinner should be ready in about fifteen minutes. Wash ya hands."

Malik was stuffed. He sat on the couch slumped over. His eyes fluttered; the itis had caught hold of him. The family was scattered throughout the home as "Cloud Nine" by the Temptations played. Unlike his brother, he enjoyed the time he spent with his family.

He had no ill feelings toward them. When their mom was sick, they weren't around because they had problems of their own. Life was hard for everyone. Malik understood that. Marcus didn't.

"Malik, can I play temple run?" his toddler cousin Lionel asked. He had cake crumbs around his mouth.

"It's about to die. I'll have to charge it first, ok? Then you can play with it."

"Oh 'kay." Lionel walked off with a smile, his hands clasped behind his back.

Poor kid, Malik thought to himself. He would be homeless in a few weeks if his Aunt Debbie didn't find the money to pay rent. She was recently laid off from her job and struggled to find work to support her family, including her grandson Lionel. After all, not many people were hiring 64-year-old women. It made Malik sad.

The emotion snapped him out of the itis. He leaned forward and massaged his forehead with both hands until his phone vibrated in his pocket. A new notification from Chase informed him he had received three thousand and seventy-one dollars through QuickPay, the exact amount their Aunt Debbie needed to avoid eviction. The money came from Marcus, and the note read: *Do the right thing.*

Malik smiled. It was a long shot and he didn't expect it, but his brother showed a rare soft spot.

"Lionel, you still wanna play that game?" Malik called his younger cousin to come to him.

"Yes!" Lionel replied with excitement as he made his way back.

After dinner at the Thompson residence, the family scattered throughout the house. Raven and Simone sat in a cozy, quiet sunroom, so they could talk.

"I went to U of I for undergrad and UC for law school because my childish ass didn't wanna be too far from home. Don't get me wrong, they're great schools of course, but the next degree I get will definitely be from an HBCU," Raven explained while sipping wine.

"That's dope. I always wanted to be one of them Spelman or Howard chicks."

"Go for it. You know Rich went to Benedict in South Carolina for a year."

"Yea, he told me about that kinda, but it's too late for me now. I'm twenty-four."

"It's never too late. You're just a year younger than me. Don't think like that, boo. Plus, you can pay your way through school for the most part with yo dancing skills. I heard about that split move."

Simone's eyes widened. She almost choked on her wine. "Oh my God! Rich didn't tell you about that, did he?"

"It's cool. I ain't tripping. I don't judge you, and you don't seem like the 'typical' stripper. My brother really likes you. He hasn't been like this in a long time."

"Thank you, Raven. I really like him too. I love him. I plan on giving my all to help him build this business, and then I won't have to dance no more."

"Y'all storybook ending is coming soon. Now tell me how I can get my abs like that though!"

Meanwhile, the Thompson men were in Roland's study.

Roland turned to Rich. "So, you secured funding for your 'lil business venture, huh? Who backed you?"

"Yea I did. An associate of mine backed me. The business has grown rapidly. We have already secured orders from retailers in the Midwest."

"That's great. I'm happy to hear that, Rich. I knew you could do it," Robert said.

"I hope you see this one through. Don't ruin it like the others," Roland said.

"Trust me, I won't. In about three years this business will grow and you will see. I'll show you."

Roland turned his attention to Robert. "You got any information on this new investor that bought out Marid and Jay?"

"Nah, I don't pop. The company is a mystery. All we know is the name is Urban Capital."

"They haven't been to any quarterly meetings yet. I don't like being in the dark."

"Ain't you retiring next year? Why does it matter who they are?" Rich asked.

"Because a good king is familiar with anyone that enters the kingdom. Let me ask you this Richard. Why you bring that girl here?"

Robert sensed the incoming conflict and attempted to interject. "Dad, come on now."

"Your mama don't know that girl is a damn hooker, but you still shouldn't of brought her here."

"She's not a hooker. She's a dancer, and she's my girlfriend. That's why I brought her. What the hell is the issue?"

"No issue at all. Just curious to know why my son is in love with a damn whore. That ain't no career. Shaking ass and fucking for money."

"I just told your ass she ain't no fucking hoe. Don't fucking disrespect her again." Rich stepped toward his father. Robert stood up to separate them and diffuse the situation, but it was too late.

"Boy, are you stepping to me?" Roland asked. The father and son stood toe-to-toe, staring each other down.

"Fuck you, Roland! You ain't my mothafucking father. You ain't shit but a greedy ass piece of shit. I will be better than you. Mark my words."

"You better watch what you say to me boy."

"Fuck you bitch ass nigga!" With that statement, Rich stormed out the room.

When he got to the first floor, he went straight to Simone. "Grab your things. Let's go, we're leaving."

Simone frowned. "What? Why?"

"Yea, what's going on Rich? We're having a good convo," Raven said.

"I said grab your coat. Let's go," Rich screamed.

Gloria walked into the room. "What's all of this commotion about?"

Rich tossed Simone her coat. "Love you mama, but we gotta go."

"Dammit, what is going on?" Gloria demanded.

Robert came downstairs. "Rich! Come on man, let's talk this out."

"Rob, what happened?" Leah asked, but he ignored her.

"Oh my God, Robert what happened? What is going on?" Raven asked. The entire family was in disbelief.

"It ain't shit to talk about. Fuck him! It's war from here on out." Rich grabbed Simone by the arm, and the couple walked out the door.

"Baby, what is going on? What happened?" Simone demanded as they stormed down the long driveway. Robert, Raven, and Leah along with other family members rushed out the house after them, but they were too far behind to catch the couple. Rich sped off immediately. Roland watched from an upstairs window with glee.

"My father, my piece of shit father. Fuck him! I hate him. I hate that mothafucka."

Simone rubbed the back of Rich's neck. "Oh my God! What did he do to make you so upset?"

"He disrespected me for the last time. Now it's over." Rich ignored multiple calls from his family. "I will never let anyone disrespect you or myself. It's just us against the world. I don't care no more, and I prefer it that way."

Thanksgiving at Dezi's house was less dramatic.

"When will the actual ceremony be?" Mrs. Winters asked Dezi and Dion while they were eating dessert.

"We haven't decided on that just yet," Dion responded.

She smiled. "Y'all been married for almost a year now. I want to be a proud mother at a ceremony, and I want my grandchildren."

"Mom, please not now. We will figure it out. We're married, and that's all that matters. The courthouse was perfect for us," Dezi said.

The two met in New York where Dion was a reporter. After dating for six months, he asked Dezi to marry him. Shortly after they married, he was offered a weekend meteorologist spot in Chicago, which so happened to be her hometown. It was a win for both of them, until she ran into Marcus at the grocery store—the last person she wanted to see. Not because she didn't want to see him, but because she didn't need to see him. She still had strong feelings for him. She also had regrets of breaking up with him and leaving cold turkey years ago. She felt bad about it and wanted to make things right, but how could she? She was married now. Dezi wasn't frustrated in her marriage with Dion, but she wanted more. She needed more.

After dinner at her parent's house, they went back to the home Dion rented—a respectable quad-level home in the northern suburbs of Chicago.

"Your family is hilarious. I love being around them," Dion said.

"I'm glad you do."

Dion grabbed the back of her head and kissed her. "I love you, Desire."

"I love you too."

Raven had been calling her brother all day to hear his side of the story. She knew Rich and her father always had issues, but she never knew it would explode like this. Furthermore, she was frustrated that the man she had been dating for an entire year failed to show up to another family function. She had plans to go out, but she was mentally drained. She was lying in bed wrapped in her bath towel when she got a text.

Open the door.

Raven was puzzled because she lived in a high-rise condo building in the Streeterville neighborhood, conveniently owned by D.T. King. There was a security check-in downstairs, so there was no way he could have made his way upstairs without them buzzing her. She hurried to the door and opened it. There stood Malik holding a sweet potato pie.

He walked inside. "I told you I was gonna bring one of my aunt's pies. You gonna love it."

"So now you show up? And how did you get past security?"

"He let me in. He knows me by now."

"That ain't the point." She strutted away from him. "Lock the door."

"Why you so feisty?"

"Cause Lameer, you stood me up again! Why don't you wanna meet my family? What are you scared of?"

"I'm not afraid of anything. I promise. It's just that I had a family crisis today. My aunt was on the verge of being evicted, so I had to help them out." His explanation was partially true. But he couldn't reveal that he and his brother were trying to take over her family business.

"I'm sorry to hear that." Raven sighed and sat down. "Today has been a disaster."

Malik rubbed her thigh. "Why? What happened?"

"My dad and my brother just can't get along at all. They got into a huge argument after dinner. It was bad. I don't think they will ever be close again."

"How bad? Like it can't be repaired at all?"

Raven let out a sigh. "I doubt it. If it is repaired, it won't be the same. Things will never be the same."

Malik engulfed her into his arms. "I'm sorry baby. I really am."

"I guess it's a good thing you weren't there. I don't want you to witness that."

"Well, I'm here now. With you. I love you baby, and we still have a lot to be thankful for."

Malik kissed her. Raven felt chills. Every time Malik touched her, she couldn't control herself. She felt her sweet spot soak instantly, and at that point, she was calm again.

Marcus spent the majority of his Thanksgiving evening at the craps table drinking. He was tipsy and had blown hundreds of dollars at that point. He was in a daze as he witnessed a couple across the room having fun together, like how he and Dezi used to have fun. She wasn't good for his health and he knew it, but he couldn't get her out of his mind. He had to remain focused on the task at hand—which was to assume full ownership of D.T. King. That was the *only* goal.

"Sir. It's your roll," the table master said, snapping Marcus out of his daze. Marcus swallowed the last gulp of his Remy and tossed the dice.

"Five. Point!" the table master screamed. And just like that, Marcus knew he would always win no matter what.

Chapter 10

"You can't be a good businessman and a saint..."

"THERE WILL BE SCATTERED SNOW showers throughout the area well into the night. Come Monday, however, we will be back in sunny skies and the mid-twenties," Dion said as he read his teleprompter.

Elliot watched the weather report from the comfort of his home. It was the middle of December, and it already looked like a white Christmas. The doorbell rang to his surprise. He got up off the sofa and slipped into his house shoes. He made his way to the door. The FedEx man stood there with a package in his hand.

"Mr. Briggs?"

"Yes, that's me."

"Can you sign here for me, sir?" The deliveryman handed the device to him. Once Elliot signed it, he handed over the package and left. Elliot was puzzled at the package until he realized it was from Robert. He sat down and opened the unexpected gift, a twenty-five thousand-dollar bottle of Gleddifich whiskey scotch.

Elliot frowned. Their battle intensified.

Marcus knew something was wrong with Rich at their monthly meeting. He was not himself.

"Rich, you alright?"

"Yea, I'm cool. Just got a lot on the mind, that's all."

"Do you want to talk about it? The business is moving up fast, and you gotta be on your A-game."

"Baby, I'm bout to head out," Simone said, interrupting their meeting. She looked at Marcus. "Excuse me."

"No problem at all. You guys have your moment." Marcus walked over to the window to check his phone.

"Don't worry about him baby. Get him out of your head," Simone told Rich. "It was weeks ago. As long as you focus on him, he is winning, and he won't win. *We* will win."

"You right, we will win. Fuck him. I'm over it, and the only way to go is up from here."

Simone kissed him. Marcus stood in the background to give them their privacy. Once Simone exited, he sat back down.

"So, what's the issue?"

"My father's a piece of shit. He disrespected me too many times, and now he disrespected my woman. It's time to bury him."

Marcus leaned forward in interest.

"Has your relationship always been like this with your father?"

"Yea, since I was a teenager. He's overbearing, and he doesn't know how to extend grace or forgive. He expects all of us to follow in his footsteps and do what he has done. He fails to realize that maybe that's not what we want, at least that's not what I want."

"Mmm-hmmm," Marcus said as he let Rich vent.

"My brother Rob…man I love him, but he ain't nothing but my dad's pet. He does whatever he says. He can't think for himself. My sister is the baby. She's spoiled. She never had intentions on working for the family business. She wants to be a judge. I never bowed down to dad, and the real estate business is boring to me. I wanted to do other shit, you know? But instead of supporting me, he bashes me at every turn. I mean, yea I fucked up. I fucked up a lot in my early years, but shit. I'm human, what the fuck? It's just a lot man. Real talk. But fuck him."

"Who do you think he loves most out of you three?"

"Shit, I would say no one, especially since the company isn't in the will."

"What you mean?"

"The business, D.T. King. He's not leaving that shit to nobody. That's his *favorite* child. I'm sure he's leaving us all some money here and there, but he ain't leaving the business to none of us, not even my mama. That shit going to his partners."

"Well, the best revenge is success. Why did he disrespect your girl?"

"Cause she's a stripper. He believes she's a hoe, but Simone is nothing like that."

"Yea, she doesn't seem like it at all."

"Ima marry that girl. I'm planning on proposing next summer before her birthday."

"You gonna invite your dad?"

"Nope."

Marcus chuckled. "Well, fuck him. Keep focusing on Nubian Noir."

"It's about time someone tells me what's going on," Roland demanded.

Roland didn't mind small shareholders selling, but with Marid Jabbar selling his stake in the firm, it gave the new investor Urban Capital a lot of skin in the game, and most importantly, *his* company.

"Why is everyone so eager to sell now? If they want to sell, then it needs to be in-house. No more outside investors."

"A young buck named Vince Brown is the registered agent. He has a lot of money to play with. But they can't get any further. Our remaining partners will never sell. We are alright," William explained.

"Is there something you're not telling me, William?" Roland asked.

"Why are you asking that?"

"The Indianapolis project, all of our partners selling so suddenly. Something isn't adding up. And I'm going to figure it out. I want to meet this Vince Brown guy."

William began to sweat. He did hold back one crucial fact—Marcus Dreer was the main insurgent.

Can we talk?

Marcus looked at the text on his phone. He felt played by Dezi, yet again. Since she revoked the invite for Thanksgiving, she had become distant. He wasn't sure what she was hiding from him, but he knew it was something.

Sure.

She told him she would stop by his house later that evening at eight p.m. Dezi was his drug. He couldn't leave her alone, although he believed it would be best for him.

Dezi pulled up at 7:58 p.m. exactly. Marcus let her in and then sat down on his couch without speaking a word.

"Hey," she said.

"What's up? What did you want to talk about?"

"How was your Thanksgiving? Was it nice?"

"Desirè, just please spit it out."

"I'm sorry I reneged on my invitation for Thanksgiving. It's just that…" Dezi paused. "I haven't been honest with you about Dion."

"Y'all are in a relationship, huh? I knew it. I could just tell by the way he looked at you. I felt it." Marcus tried to contain his disappointment.

"We're married."

"What?"

"We're married, Marcus."

"That's your fucking husband! Are you serious right now?"

He got up and paced around to gather his thoughts. "You can leave now. Say no more." Dezi tried to reach toward him, but Marcus moved his arm.

"I said you can leave! Get out of here. Don't worry about locking the door." He walked away from her into his bedroom.

Dezi followed him into the room. Marcus sat on the edge of the bed with his face buried in his hands. He was tired of her playing with his emotions. Dezi sat on the opposite side of the bed. No one spoke for a while.

Marcus eventually broke the silence. "You shouldn't be here."

"But I am," Dezi said with guilt in her voice. "I'm here because I love *you* Marcus. Only you. I've loved you since we were fourteen years old. I've made many mistakes in my life, and I haven't been the best, but the truth is I want you. Not him."

"Then why did you marry him?"

"Because that was one of my many mistakes."

Marcus stood up and faced her. Dezi looked back at him with tears in her eyes.

"I refuse to love another man's wife. If you want me the way you say you do, then you have to end it with him. Otherwise, I don't want to see you at all. If I never see you again, then I know what it is."

"Okay." Dezi stood up and kissed him on the lips and then turned to leave. Before she could take a step, Marcus pulled her back and threw her on the bed. Dezi unbuckled her pants while Marcus removed her shoes and then pulled off her jeans. Once they were on the floor, he stopped and stared into her eyes. He felt Dezi's heart beating out of her chest.

Dezi and Marcus had sex countless times. However, something about this time felt different. It was as if Marcus was claiming his territory, and he sensed she loved it. When Marcus thrusted his manhood in her, it felt like he touched her soul.

Raven was knocked out. As she laid on her stomach, her rich chocolate melanin glowed beautifully underneath the blue lights in her ceiling. Raven and Malik had been going all night, and the last round put her down for the count. Malik peeked back in to check on her. He went to the kitchen to get a glass of water once he saw Raven asleep, and then he headed to the living room. He walked up to her high windows and surveyed the city. The beautiful night sky filled with lights made him smile. The light snowflakes dancing in the air were gorgeous.

"Simple. It all could be so simple," Malik whispered to himself. He loved Raven, he *genuinely* loved her. But how much longer could he live in secret? No, he wasn't cheating on her, but he was hiding who he *really* was. Raven didn't know him, his background, or his family, and she certainly didn't know his brother. From the day they first met, he went by his middle name, Lameer. How could he tell the woman he loved that she was related to his enemy?

Eleven months prior, Malik, his best friend Israel aka Izzy, and a few others went on vacation to Cabo San Lucas. One evening in the hotel lobby while drinking with the crew, Malik noticed a gorgeous chocolate woman watching him from across the way. Her hair was in a bun, and she wore a lovely orange romper. Her sunglasses rested on her head.

Izzy observed the game of chess the two were playing and how they continued to give each other looks when the other wasn't watching. "You betta go get her and quit playing before I do!" he said as he paid for another round of drinks. He passed one to Malik. Malik grabbed the glass, but kept his eyes focused on Raven the entire time.

"I'm 'bout to go talk to her."

"My nigga!" Izzy cheered him on.

Malik sat down next to Raven at the bar as she chatted with her friends. Raven knew why he came over. She was happy, but she acted oblivious.

"How you doing?" Malik asked, interrupting Raven's conversation. She looked back at him over her left shoulder.

"I'm good, and yourself?"

"I can't compl..." Malik's sentence was cut short when he attempted to place his drink on the bar but miscalculated. His drink fell to the ground. Liquor and glass splashed everywhere.

Malik jumped up and scrambled to look for something to clean up the mess he had just made. "Fuck, fuck! I'm sorry. You ok?"

Izzy turned his head away and laughed from across the way.

"Oh my God," Raven whispered as she looked down at her sandals. Her feet were wet, but she was okay. "I'm fine." Her friends got up and walked away laughing, leaving Raven alone with her clumsy stranger.

"I'm sorry. I don't know how the hell that happened."

"It's ok, sir. It is." Raven stepped away from the bar to get herself together. A hotel custodian came to clean up the mess Malik created.

"Can I buy you another drink?"

"My drink is over there on the bar. *You're* the one that needs a drink."

Malik was embarrassed. "Damn, I'm tweaking."

"Um, are you ok? You drunk? Maybe you don't need another drink."

"Yea, I'm ok," he said. "I just need some fresh air."

"Yea, you do that."

Dejected, Malik began to walk toward the door for some fresh air, but something inside him clicked. He refused to lose that easy. He wanted her, and he would get her.

He turned around. "You're very beautiful. We been in Mexico

for two days so far, and you're by far the most beautiful woman I've seen. I came over here to get to know you, and somehow that got fucked up. I still wanna get to know you actually, and all I'm asking for is a chance. We don't need any drinks. Let's just go walk in the sand and talk."

Raven stood with her arms folded and stared at him.

"Please…" Malik said.

After two seconds, which felt like two hours to Malik, she agreed.

"Ok, come on." She walked ahead of him leading the way. Malik followed her closely.

They made their way outside on the beach. The cool breeze was refreshing. Raven stepped in the sand and removed her sandals.

"Is this your first time in Mexico?" she asked, breaking the silence.

"Yea it is. Is it yours?"

"Nah, this is maybe my tenth time. I'm not sure. I lost count."

"Well damn! You got it like that, huh?" Malik was impressed, a little taken aback by her financial status. She had money.

"I'm a daddy's girl. It has its perks, especially when he's rich."

"What does your dad do? And does daddy's girl have a name?"

"My name is Raven, and my father owns the biggest real estate company in Chicago."

"You're from Chicago? Wow, this night just keeps getting more interesting. I am too. What's the name of the company?"

"Wow, what a coincidence. And the name is D.T. King."

Malik's shock deepened as he gazed out into the water.

"So, are you going to tell me your name, or are you going to continue to be a mystery?" she asked.

"I see you're an open book. My name is Malik, but everyone calls me Lameer."

"I answer the questions that I'm asked. And why does everyone call you Lameer?"

"Lameer is my middle name. I have no idea why everyone calls me that, but they just do," Malik said, even though it was a lie. No one called him that.

"Come on, I know the perfect place to chill right over there." She led him to a tree. They sat down and got comfortable. "I'll tell you one thing Lameer. You're persistent. I like that."

"Oh really?"

"Is this how you are with every girl you meet on vacation?"

"Nah, not at all." He chuckled. "I told you, you're the most beautiful girl I seen."

"Where are you from specifically back home?" she asked, changing the subject.

"Markham. And yourself?"

"Beverly."

"Yea, you definitely rich."

"I told you I'm not rich. My daddy is. I just spend his money."

"You're not stuck up I see."

"I mean I'm grateful and all of that, but I want to make my own money."

"What are your aspirations?" Malik asked.

"I'm in my second year of law school. I want to be a judge one day. Gotta start out as a lawyer first, of course."

"That's what's up. I see the authoritative figure in you. I just graduated from grad school."

"And what do you plan on doing now?"

"I'm not sure. Maybe work at my brother's lounge for a while until I figure it all out."

"You will."

"You have faith in my clumsy ass, huh?"

Raven smiled. "I ain't say all of that now. I just like to be optimistic. You are kinda cute or whatever though."

"Is that what you tell every dude you meet on vacation?"

Raven giggled. "Ok, you got me. That was a good one. I still need to pop you for spilling that long island on me."

"Well, hopefully you can buy me a new one. You got it?"

Raven and Malik talked for hours into the night about everything, from their favorite foods to their childhood dreams. Malik was lucky that Raven had the patience to see past his initial woes, and Raven was relieved that Malik didn't just want sex. They were in bliss, but Malik kept a major secret from her. A secret he is still struggling to reveal to her eleven months later. The truth. No one called him Lameer, in fact, he honestly hated his middle name. He only told Raven that to keep his true lineage at bay.

"Yes, it's been a long time." Roland Thompson exhaled the cigar smoke and studied it as it floated toward the ceiling. "But I still remember every step of the way. What keeps you going? Why do you always want more?" he asked Elliot.

Roland was enjoying a cigar while Elliot sat across from him in his office. It was part of Roland's vetting process to see if Elliot was worthy of becoming the next CEO. They were discussing many things—business, success stories, life.

Elliot coughed from the smoke. "Well to be frank Mr. Thompson, what keeps me going is God."

"I see. Tell me more."

Elliot helped himself to a glass of water to soothe his throat. "Are you familiar with the Tefillah?"

"I'm not."

"It began in the Jewish tradition and made its way into Christianity. It's the daily practice of praying three times a day. The morning is called the Shacharit, being grateful to see another day. The afternoon is called the Mincha, giving a daily sacrifice. And lastly, the Maariv is the evening prayer, which is when God reveals himself even in the darkest hours."

"Beautiful."

"I say all of that to say this…In business, I truly believe God entrusts everything to us. None of this is ours. Our success isn't ours. It's his. So, my motivation to continue to rise to the top and do greater things is not for myself. It's for his glory. To do his will. I'm just a servant."

Roland nodded his head in admiration. "That's a good perspective. Damn good, might I add."

"What motivates you?" Elliot asked.

Roland took a sip of brandy after a long pull from his stick. "Having more motivates me. I remember this stubborn bastard from a long time ago. His name was Maurice Edwards. He wouldn't sell me his ten-unit apartment building. The property was terrible, and the old man couldn't afford to keep it up, so why not just sell and be done with it, right? Nevertheless, he refused. He decided to play hard ball. I noticed a safety hazard in one of the units, and I threatened to tell the city officials if he didn't get it fixed. Again, he refused. I convinced the tenant to sue him if I paid for the court costs. God, I was ruthless then."

Elliot's raised his eyebrow as Roland continued.

"I knew this bastard didn't have the funds to fight a long court case. It wasn't long before he begged me to stop. He even said he would sell the building for less value. He died less than a year later." Roland's eyes stared into space as if he was reliving the moment. "Stupid old man. Now that entire neighborhood belongs to D.T. King. You will see D.T. King signage everywhere. He could have been rich and rode off into sunset. His grandkids could've lived off his proceeds, but he wanted to resist. He wanted to be stupid."

"Interesting," Elliot replied.

"I'm motivated by power. I believe it's my job to cleanse this industry of the weak. Black, white, it doesn't matter. They all will lose just the same. You can't be a good businessman and a saint Elliot. Something must be sacrificed."

CHAPTER 11
1985

S AM DREER MADE HIS WAY to Chicago in 1967 at the tender
age of thirteen. He came from St. Louis, Missouri to live
with his Uncle Eddie. His parents put him on a train and
sent him on his way so that their son could have a better chance at
life.

Uncle Eddie lived in the Bronzeville neighborhood on the South
Side of Chicago. Sam wasn't a super intelligent boy. He attended
DuSable High School, which was the best 'Negro' high school in
the city. He struggled with most of the subjects, especially math,
but he was determined to make something of himself. However,
he did excel in woodshop. Sam was great with his hands, and he
amazed his teachers. His uncle raved to the neighborhood about
his ability to construct things. It wasn't long before Sam started
building dressers, tables, or anything else his neighbors needed
help with. After he graduated college, Sam worked minor jobs to
help his uncle but continued his freelance work until he saved up
enough money.

Sam's twenty-first birthday in 1975 was the best year of his life.

He married Terri, his sweetheart and best friend. Terri was the
most beautiful woman in the world to Sam, and he chose her to
be his wife. A prominent local business-man approached Sam later
that year and asked him to build his new home. He was aware
of Sam's skills and offered to pay him more money than he had

ever seen in his life. Thus, a business was born. Dreer Properties &
Construction was only the beginning.

The couple purchased a home in Markham. Sam wanted a
family desperately because he never had one, but they were unable
to conceive a child. Sam just put his faith in God and believed it
would happen when the time was right.

Business grew thanks to his first contract and connections.
The more business boomed, the more Sam had to hire others.
His young firm grew when 1978 hit. That's when he hired on a
young ambitious man named Roland Thompson to do the in-house
accounting.

Roland was the same age as Sam. A former college football star,
Roland had gotten hurt, which ruined all hopes of him going to
the NFL. He was depressed, but he figured he had to find another
league to enter, so he chose real estate. Roland impressed Sam a
lot and quickly gained his trust, especially since he made things
more cost efficient for the business. In 1981, Sam made Roland a
partner. The firm's new name was D.T. King Properties Inc. Dreer
and Thompson were the kings of development, but it was clear the
real force behind the company was Sam Dreer.

Sam had vision, and he was the man with the plan. Sam was
even featured in *Ebony* magazine. Roland wasn't invited to the
photo shoot. He was always used to being the man, but that time
he was the sidekick. And he didn't like it.

The jealousy and envy boiled in Roland's spirit. It finally
climaxed when someone referred to Sam as his boss. Roland
exploded. He started plotting at that moment. Roland was a shrewd
man, and he demanded respect at all costs.

His plotting cultivated with an internal hostile takeover in
1985. Sam was blindsided and bought out. Furious and stunned,
Sam fought it. But due to the loopholes in the company's bylaws,
there was nothing he could do.

A month later on May 30, 1985, Sam and Terri finally gave birth to their first child, Marcus. Sam took Roland to court, and after a one-year battle, he was awarded a miniscule six-figure settlement. It was another slap in the face. The company he started grossed far more than that. Sam was dejected for a long time. He continued his contracting work, but Roland took his entrepreneurial spirit. Sam purchased a strip mall. His first tenant was a man named Carl Fulton who had a great recipe for wings. Other businesses came and went over the years.

Sam's settlement and savings were all he had left after Roland stole D.T. King from him. The plaza kept the bills paid, and whenever he got a gig to rehab a house, it was extra money. However, things were much harder than they had been the previous ten years. Roland and D.T. King had sewn up most of the potential clientele Sam could contract. As a result, Sam was shut out of the business, and things quickly dried up for him. The plaza became the only source of income for him.

In 1992, Terri gave birth to their second child, Malik. However, she was diagnosed with cervical cancer not long after that. Sam committed every penny he had to her treatment, but after a two-year long battle, she passed. Sam and young Marcus were devastated.

From that point on Marcus became his father's helping hand—taking care of Malik, helping out with the plaza, doing everything he could to ease the burden off his father's shoulders. That was the world Marcus grew up in. He had to grow up fast. There was no time to be a kid. As a result, he latched on to the entrepreneurial spirit strongly. He accompanied his dad on rehab projects.

Marcus was a good student at East Markham High School, but unfortunately, he did not qualify for a scholarship. He received financial aid and attended Northern Illinois University, so he could be close to home. During winter break of his sophomore year, his father told him the truth about Roland Thompson and D.T. King and how Roland screwed him out of the business *he built*. Sam was a man of integrity and trusted Roland, so he was completely blindsided. He urged his son to always do business with integrity and avoid the naïve mistakes he made. He told him that family must always remain first.

From that moment, a fire burned deep inside Marcus, a fire of rage with a thirst for vengeance. How could a man do this to a person he considered a friend? Ruin his business career and remove him from the company he started? Marcus immediately blamed Roland Thompson for all of the misfortune his family suffered. And Marcus wanted revenge.

He began to concoct a plan to take back his father's company. He didn't return to school after his sophomore year. Sam was against it, but Marcus insisted on handling the day-to-day operations of the strip plaza. He worked full-time with his father, managing the plaza and looking for rehab gigs. With Marcus' tenacity, they secured more gigs. But Marcus moved in silence and wouldn't rest until he took D.T. King back and made Roland Thompson pay.

Tragedy struck again in 2008 when Sam died. Marcus concluded his father died from a broken heart. Marcus and Malik were left alone. Two brothers against the world. Marcus followed his father's wishes and made sure Malik got a scholarship. Malik earned his Bachelor's and his Master's degree. After grad school, he helped his brother full-time with the plaza.

Malik knew what had happened to his father as well. Malik wanted payback like his brother, but Malik was different. Not as hot-headed, Malik preferred diplomatic approaches to all conflicts in life—which was the only reason he held back when he met Raven that fateful night in Cabo San Lucas. She was the daughter of a snake, but her beauty was much more intoxicating than the venom. Malik didn't want to associate her with Roland. He wanted to focus on her and only her, so he did. He knew his brother wouldn't support the relationship at all, so he kept it hidden from him. Raven bought him the watch and helped him get his credit repaired to purchase the new car. Raven was his world, but she was in the dark. It was the reason he refused to meet her family.

Meanwhile Marcus' plan was in motion. He had gained a noticeable foothold in the company thanks to the partnership of his loyal friend Vince. But he needed confirmation on one more thing. There was one more piece to the puzzle, and it would all be complete.

CHAPTER 12

"I CAN GET USED TO THIS."

"**O**H MY GOD, DEEPER," ADJOA moaned as Vince stroked her. Her legs were wrapped tightly around his back. He stroked her in circles nonstop as she continued to moan. Her eyes rolled all the way to the back of her head when Vince sucked on her neck.

"I'm coming. Oh, fuck I'm coming," she screamed. Her legs started shaking uncontrollably, but Vince continued to dig deeper in her.

Adjoa used to only stay in Chicago for a weekend at the most, but since she met Vince, she stayed an entire week for him. The tryst they had the previous summer developed into an affair. Adjoa had long money. She also had her hands in real estate, but her portfolio was more diverse. She owned franchises on the east coast, as well as property. She was a major shareholder in a company that had government contracts.

Adjoa rented out a penthouse in Chicago and told Vince to come home to her, not his wife. Adjoa gave Vince peace. Vince always showed up like clockwork for his monthly rendezvous with his new mistress. He always gave her what she was looking for. It was more than sex though. Vince actually *enjoyed* his time with her. He felt he could truly be himself. There was no need to mask things as he did with Janelle.

Dezi cut through the steak methodically without saying a word. She and Dion were enjoying a fancy and upscale dinner at a steakhouse on the North Side. Dion sensed something was wrong.

"What's wrong baby?" He rested his left hand on top of hers.

"I don't know." Dezi paused before she continued. "Do you ever wonder if we rushed things?"

"Um no. Why do you ask that?"

"Because I do," Dezi said.

Dion removed his hand as he sat back and stared at her. "Desirè what are you talking about?"

"I want a divorce Dion."

Dion's face went blank. "I don't understand...Dezi what is going on?"

"I don't want to continue doing this. I want a divorce. I made a mistake marrying you. I'm sorry. It's my fault for leading you on this long."

Dion leaned forward shaking with anger.

"Dezi, I need some fuckin' answers. What has gotten into you? Why are you saying this stupid shit?" he whispered through clenched teeth.

"I just gave you the answer. The truth is I never wanted to marry you, and I don't know why I did. I made a mistake. I played with your emotions, and I'm sorry. Now I would like to end this before things continue to get worse."

Dezi stood up and started walking away. Before she exited the restaurant, she stopped and turned around. "I'll be staying at my mother's house. I'll come by this weekend to get my things, so leave your key".

Dion was stunned. Angry. "Desirè come back here!" he shouted. Everyone in the restaurant turned to see the commotion. "Come back here Desirè," he repeated himself, but it was pointless. She was gone.

Dezi immediately hopped in the Uber she ordered discreetly at the table. She hung her head in shame. Dion was a good guy. He never did anything to her. She felt horrible for what she just did to him, but she felt she had no choice if she wanted to be with the man she loved. Her phone began buzzing with incoming calls from her soon-to-be ex-husband. She put her phone on airplane mode and let the sound of the radio soothe her.

"Her work ethic is quite impressive," Angelo told Rich as they observed the staff.

Rich stared at his woman in admiration. "Yes, it is. She's a hustler for sure."

Simone didn't have an official title in the business. She just did whatever she felt needed to be done to help. Her strength was in the creative side as she expressed. She shadowed the designers and gave them her tips and input. She and Angelo discussed various strategies as well. Since the business had picked up, she wasn't dancing much. Her passion to help Rich build his empire was growing by the minute. They would be a power couple in business soon enough.

"Merry Christmas. You're finishing this year off on the right foot. Next year will be much bigger," Angelo said. He patted Rich on the back and walked off. Rich soaked in those words because he felt next year would be major, one way or another.

"Eight hundred and fifty square feet is a perfect size for your business," Malik explained to a potential tenant for the strip mall property in Markham. Carl's chicken shack and Dreams were the jewel of the property, but everything else was an eye sore. The last client to occupy the space was a beauty store, and that business went bankrupt. Since then, the property had so much vacant space.

Malik figured out a solution. He borrowed Vince's idea and decided to break the space up into smaller units. As property manager, he finally found that managerial void he'd been missing. He had occupied three out of the five units thus far and had a sense of urgency to fill the last two. Marcus was solely focused on D.T. King and Vince focused on growing organic capital for the business, so Malik took over the strip mall. He just needed to tell Marcus and Vince his plans, and they would supply the funds.

Malik was on the premises almost every day. He even brought Raven to Dreams a few times, and she loved Carl's chicken as everyone did.

"I like what I see. It's nice and compact. Just what I need," Mr. Rowell said. He was a tall thin-framed dark-skinned man with glasses in search of office space for his life insurance firm.

"Mr. Rowell, let me know if you have any questions. Don't hesitate to give me a call. Anything you need, I got you," Malik said.

Mr. Rowell shook his hand. "I will certainly be calling you sooner than later."

Malik walked into Dreams. Izzy sat on the VIP couches watching SportsCenter.

"Sherri, let me get a Corona," Malik asked the loyal bartender. He sat at the bar and checked his phone.

"So, how it go?" she asked him.

He took a swig of his beer. "Real well. I got a feeling he will be calling this afternoon."

"Man, bro I'm telling you we need to make one of them units a recording studio," Izzy said.

"An eight-hundred-square foot recording studio, dude? That shit is a closet. It ain't enough room for all that."

"Bro, it's no different than these rappers spitting in their basement. The money is there."

"Nah. Just stick to selling ounces and cracking cards. I got this." Malik tipped his beer in Izzy's direction and answered his phone. "Hello?"

"Hey Malik. It's me, Mr. Rowell. You know what, Ima just go ahead and send over my security deposit now. The location is prime, and I don't wanna miss this opportunity."

"Alright, no problem Mr. Rowell. I'll have that lease drafted up and sent to you by tomorrow."

Malik hung up the phone and motioned toward the bartender. "Sherri, let me get another one. I can get used to this."

Robert stared at the diagram on the table before him—a building with three vertical towers. It looked like a bar chart—the tower on the far left was the shortest with rooftop amenities, such as a pool, green space, and lounges. The tower on the right was slightly taller, while the middle right tower was the tallest of them all.

"Wow. What a design this is," Robert said.

Roland stared at the diagram in awe. "She's beautiful, isn't she? I've been planning this for a long, *long* time. Son, I purchased that plot of land back in '95. It's taken me years to find the right team, the right engineers, and the right architect. I hired a woman-owned firm to create this rendering. I proposed this a few years ago, but that damn alderman rejected me. This new alderman is on our side. This is why friendship is important."

He rubbed his fingers together. "One King's Square is the name. This will be my magnum opus as a real estate developer. You're looking at a unique one-hundred story skyscraper that will be complete by the year 2021. Once it's finished, it will be the second tallest building in Chicago. Over four hundred and ten luxury condos all being sold for a minimum of a million dollars. Plus, a two hundred and twelve room five-star hotel. All of this is the brainchild of a Black-owned company. The Plan Commission approved it last week."

"Damn pop. This is unbelievable. I'm speechless."

"I remember when I hosted a fundraiser event for Harold Washington when he ran for re-election. The city was alive back then, especially the Black communities. Now this city has no identity anymore. This tower will bring Chicago back to the forefront, and it will inspire the Black community cause it's 'niggers' that built it and they said, 'niggers' can't do anything."

"We've been proving people wrong since the beginning of time."

"Yes, we have. I have a team of bankers from Shanghai that have a keen interest in loaning us half of the costs to break ground on this. Eight hundred and fifty million to be exact. They are eager to meet."

"I'm sure you will close the deal dad," Robert said.

Roland looked at him. "Not me. You. I'm retiring this year, remember? I will remain the chairman and top shareholder, but I won't be on the front line anymore. I had the vision, but you will bring it to fruition. I want you to finish it."

Robert was shocked and humbled. "I'm honored dad. I really am. I won't let you down."

"This competition between you and Elliot was a serious evaluation, however, you're my son, my blood. I trust you with this task. You close this deal, and you will be my successor. No questions asked."

Robert was ecstatic. He could finally see the light at the end of the tunnel. He was finally about to take the reign of the family business.

As soon as Vince walked into his house, the aroma of shrimp and lobster met him at the door, which surprised him because Janelle rarely cooked. The smell instantly made him hungry. It didn't take him long to realize the kids were not at home either. He walked into the kitchen and stared at Janelle for a few moments. She turned around and jumped.

"Oh my god! I didn't hear the door open at all. How long have you been standing there?" She clutched her chest.

"Not long. I see you back in the kitchen, huh?" He glanced at the shrimp sizzling in the skillet. "What's the special occasion? Where's the kids?"

"Just wanted to do something nice for you, that's all. The kids are at my parent's house." She kissed him on the lips. Vince knew something was different. Maybe she was turning over a new leaf. "I wanted to do something special for you tonight."

The couple enjoyed the home-cooked dinner and wine. The date night was refreshing. Vince was so used to coming home to a war zone filled with negativity, he wasn't sure if tonight was real.

After dinner, Janelle led him into the bedroom where they proceeded to make love. After they finished, Vince cradled her in his arms.

She caressed his chest. "I'm sorry."

"For what?"

"Everything. Stressing you out. Not being there for you. Refusing to attend couples therapy with you."

Vince had attended monthly therapy sessions for the past two years. His battle with depression and anxiety started in his teenage years. Some storms were worse than others. That last job he had at WestGate stressed him out to the core, and Janelle's ungratefulness and unhappiness drove him to the brink. He decided to take up therapy for himself and asked her to attend with him, but she declined because she claimed therapy wasn't needed.

"I'm also sorry for Janice."

Vince sat up on the edge of the bed after hearing her apology.

"I'm sorry Vince." Tears formed in Janelle's eyes. "Not a day goes by when I don't regret what I did. I was in high school, young and stupid. I should have never cheated on you. You still decided to forgive me and raise her as your own daughter, and I'll forever be grateful for that."

"Yea." Vince stared into the darkness ahead of him. "I think she knows I'm not her daddy. I can tell by the way she acts."

"She's like that with me too. You're the only father she has ever known. You are her father. You make sure she never goes without. You're an amazing father to all of our kids. You're an amazing husband, and I just want to let you know I appreciate you and I'm sorry. I want to fix our marriage. I want to save it."

Janelle's heartfelt apology resonated within his heart. The pain and anger from her infidelity still stung from time to time, but ultimately, he forgave her a long time ago. Vince did what most men wouldn't do—he took his girlfriend back after she cheated, and he raised a baby that wasn't his. Eventually he had two biological children of his own with her. He made a lot of sacrifices for Janelle and his family. The frustration came in because she never appreciated him, definitely not as much as he appreciated her. Maybe she noticed how Vince had withdrawn from her, and she finally came to her senses. Vince was a good man, and he was willing to make the marriage work, but it was more so for his children. However, now his heart was shared with someone else. Adjoa.

CHAPTER 13

"It's that simple huh?"

"**D**ADDY, WHEN WAS THE LAST time you worked out?" Raven asked her father.

"I work out when I can. At least two to three times a month," Roland said.

Raven stopped by her parent's house on a Sunday afternoon after church. Mama Thompson cooked her signature chili while Raven and Roland sat by the fireplace.

"It needs to be two to three times a week. Come on now, you heard what the doctor told you. You ain't getting no younger. You have to keep that heart in shape."

Roland's lack of urgency for his health at times irritated and worried Raven. She loved her parents. They were her world. Her relationship with her father, however, was unique. It was clear Roland had a soft spot for her. She was the only one who could get away with murder in his eyes. Maybe it's because he never expected her to follow in his footsteps. He always put that pressure on Robert and Rich. When Rich decided not to follow the family business, all of the weight fell on Robert's shoulders.

"Ok boss, I'll work out first thing in the morning when I get to the office. I promise."

"Good." Raven glanced at her phone. "So, when's the last time you and Rich spoke?"

"Not since Thanksgiving. Your mother talked to him a few times."

"You haven't texted him or nothing?"

"Baby girl, your brother is a very emotional man. He's always been that way since he was a child. He's thirty-one years old. He is a grown man. If he doesn't want to be around his family, then it's his decision."

"The issue isn't family; the issue is you. It's y'all two. I've spoken with him, and so has Robert and Mama. Everyone but you. I don't like y'all being at odds like this. I never saw him so mad before. And you shouldn't have called Simone what you called her."

"When he stops being sensitive, then we can talk again."

A look of disappointment crossed Raven's face.

The stress weighing on Marcus over the past few months was becoming overwhelming. He knew taking over the company wouldn't be easy. He felt so close, yet so far away. Since Marid folded, they hadn't been successful in buying any of the other partners.

"He wants to meet," Vince said as he walked in and took a seat.

Marcus leaned back into his chair "Roland?"

"Yup." Vince picked up the Rubik's cube on Marcus' desk. "He wants to know the mysterious company that's been buying up shares."

"When and where?" Marcus asked.

"His secretary called me about an hour ago to check my availability. She'll call back this afternoon with a date and time."

"Ok cool. You know how to play it right?"

"Of course," Vince said. "This means we finally got his attention, but you also know we have to move quicker than ever now. Once he finds out who we really are, he's going to counter and try to stop us."

"It won't work. I have a wild card for that. Just in case."

Vince looked puzzled for a minute.

"Marcus, Dezi is downstairs," Marquita said, interrupting their conversation.

"Ok thanks."

"She still married to that news guy?" Vince asked.

"Don't know. Don't care," Marcus said, even though he lied. He did care.

Vince smirked. "Don't beat yourself up over that man. Shit happens. At least you ain't in my situation."

"You and Adjoa really getting deep ain't y'all?"

"This shit is crazy bro. But with her I feel alive, you feel me? She cares for me, she's *interested* in me. I can't explain it."

"Janelle cheated on you when we were in high school. I guess it's karma. At the same time bro, you need to be careful. You have a lot to lose. Kids, money, reputation, all of that."

"Trust me, I know. I'm going to figure it out."

"When the last time y'all talked?"

"We talk every day. I'm going to Jersey this weekend to see her." Marcus shook his head. "Yo ass got two wives. This is unbelievable."

Dezi walked up to his office door and knocked. Vince turned around and opened the door. He greeted her with a hug.

"Dezi, how are you?"

"Hey Vince. I'm good, and yourself?"

"Just working as usual. You know how we do." He smiled and turned toward Marcus. "I'll keep you posted on that meeting time."

"Cool," Marcus said. Vince exited and closed the door.

"Can I sit?" Dezi asked.

"Um yea."

Dezi sat down and got herself situated. "The divorce should be finalized within two to three months. We met with the lawyers yesterday and everything."

"Is he still on your board of directors?"

"No, he's being removed. I want you to replace him."

"Me?"

"Yes you. I love you. I want you to be my partner in everything. I'm sorry for not being honest with you from the start."

Marcus grabbed her hands and rubbed them. "It's ok. Don't worry about the past. Let's just focus on our future."

A wave of joy crossed her face. "I wouldn't have it any other way baby."

Marcus won. He finally got the woman he always wanted back in his life and for good.

"I got a lot of work to handle down here at the strip mall with these new tenants, but I should be free around six," Malik told Raven over the phone.

"Ok, I'll hit you up after me and my siblings are done hanging out," Raven replied.

"Cool. I love you."

"Love you too, boo. Bye." Raven ended the call as she walked into the restaurant. Her two brothers awaited her at the table. The long overdue sibling day Raven yearned for had finally come.

"Well, look who's late this time," Robert joked.

"Whatever." Raven rolled her eyes and smiled.

Rich sipped his Pepsi. "Looks like the crew is back together again, huh?"

"Yes, we are." Robert took their baby sister's coat.

Raven and Rich embraced after she sat down.

"How's my sister?" she asked Robert.

"Leah's doing great. Her patient list is growing so much, they have to get a larger office soon."

"People love their pets. I shoulda became a veterinarian," Rich said.

"Yea, Leah Thompson DVM is doing just fine. She went on a shopping spree this past weekend and was generous enough to buy me this suit."

"That's so great. Congrats to her. Aww, that's cute. She really loves you. You picked the perfect wife, Robert." Raven smiled and turned to Rich. "And how is Simone? I hope she's cool. I want to see her again."

"She's doing well. She works with me full-time now."

"Oh, she doesn't dance anymore?" Raven asked.

"Nope. She was tired of it. She wants to build this business with me full force."

"That's great. I remember she was telling me something similar back at the house."

"Who financed you, Rich?" Robert changed the subject.

"Does it matter? My family didn't."

Raven rolled her eyes sensing the drama.

"You need to relax. I ain't have a million dollars to give you. If I did, I would have," Robert said.

"Your father had it."

"*Our* father," Raven interjected. "Can we please not start this, guys? Seriously."

"You broke free from your alcoholism. You couldn't get the funding at first, but you found it. You overcome the odds time after time. I have no doubt you will be successful in due time," Robert said.

"I appreciate that, seriously. I appreciate you both. At least y'all understand my madness. What's the latest with the business?"

Robert smiled. "This damn competition is finally coming to an end."

Raven tore into a piece of warm bread. "Dad loves to play mind games, that's all. I don't think he was ever going to promote that other guy to take his place."

"Did y'all know Dad is building a skyscraper?"

"A skyscraper?" Rich asked with a puzzled look on his face.

"Yes. It hasn't gone public yet, but a one-hundred story skyscraper, and he wants me to close the deal for the loan in a few weeks."

"How long has he been planning this?" Raven asked.

"For years. He really kept this one under wraps. He says it will be his magnum opus."

"This mothafucka loves to pull out surprises, doesn't he?" Rich said.

"All I have to do is close the deal, and I will be the next CEO when he steps down."

"It's that simple, huh?" Rich asked.

Robert stared at his brother for a brief moment. "Yea. It is."

"Are y'all ready to order?" Raven asked. "The server walked past us like three times."

Vince stared out the window into the sky and admired the view from the conference room. He relished this moment. His career was re-born and ignited with passion. They were taking over D.T. King bit-by-bit, and now the almighty Roland Thompson summoned him to meet. Vince knew all too well what Roland had done to Marcus and Malik's father. He didn't respect it. He didn't respect Roland, and this would be the first time he'd meet him in the flesh. Marcus had yet to meet him.

Marcus didn't make Vince the registered agent simply for espionage reasons. Marcus *knew* Vince was a better business man than himself. He trusted that Vince could make better decisions on this level, and so far, it was true. His office building project was on point; he had made the necessary connections to strengthen Urban Capital. Vince appreciated his trust, and he knew it was only the beginning.

Vince sat down in one of the chairs and leaned back. He spotted Roland walking down the hallway headed straight for the door.

"So, this is my mysterious new partner!" Roland announced in a loud voice. "Mr. Brown, it's a pleasure to finally meet you."

"Likewise, sir," Vince said.

"Oh, please call me Roland. Have they been good to you? Do you need anything? Coffee? Water?"

"No thank you. I'm totally fine."

Roland sat down. "Tell me about yourself, your business Urban Capital. Where did you guys come from?"

"I'm from here. Markham to be specific."

"Ah, South suburbs. Nice. When did you start the business?"

"Two years ago. I was tired of working for someone else, so I took a leap of faith. I spent all this money and all these years to get degrees, but here I was stuck in middle management."

"They don't care about a nigga with a degree. That's why we have to take care of our own," Roland said.

"Oh absolutely. And that's my goal."

Roland gave him an inquisitive look. "So, you took a leap of faith and boom… millions of dollars just fell into your lap?"

"It was a gift."

"That's a very big gift. Who has the leverage to do such a thing?"

Vince leaned forward with laser focus. "Santa Claus."

Roland paused for a second before he broke into laughter. "A sense of humor. I love it. You're quite the charmer young fella. So why D.T. King? What made you want to invest in my company? Marid isn't cheap. I'm still surprised he sold. I haven't heard from him since."

"I've always been interested in real estate, seeing how cities work and why they're built the way they are. Plus, it's Black-owned. I want in on that."

"You know one of my biggest goals as a real estate developer is to erase the red line."

"Fuck William Levitt."

"Oh yes, indeed. I always demand banks that partner with us to finance a certain among of minority homeowners. If they don't meet the quota, then they aren't the right fit for us."

"Is that how you got so powerful and rich?" Vince asked him.

"I got this way by playing the game. Are all white people bad? Of course not. Hell, my Vice Chairman is white as snow. But I used them as leverage."

"One of my goals is to construct a chain of community centers in the inner city that will help revitalize the youth," Vince said.

"It can be done. Is that your motivation?"

"It is. What motivates you?"

Roland leaned back in deep thought before he answered. "Wealth. I want to be the richest Black person in the history of the world.

"Mansa Musa will have something to say about that. He was the richest in the history of the world, black or white."

"Everything I touch turns to gold. How many Negros you know built a skyscraper?"

"None."

Roland flashed a proud smile. "You're looking at one, partner."

Vince smiled. "Just call me Vince. I'm not sure if you value partners."

"Are you alone? Who are you in business with?"

"I told you. Santa Claus." Vince stood up. "When will the next shareholder meeting be?"

"Next month. My birthday party is at the end of this month, but you should come and meet all of your partners informally. You will get a RSVP in the mail."

"Perfect. I look forward to it. Will I have access to the bylaws to educate myself accordingly?"

"Of course, youngster."

The two men shook hands, neither backing down from the force of manhood.

CHAPTER 14
"Stranger danger"

ROBERT HAD GONE OVER THE prospectus his team prepared repeatedly. He had done that a million times before for countless projects—shopping malls, condo rises, apartment buildings—but never for a project this huge. This building would be the second largest building in Chicago upon completion. The home of the skyscraper. The city with the best skyline in the world.

This wasn't just any other project. He and his team stood in anticipation as the bankers from Shanghai approached them. They were meeting in D.T. King's offices. His father had taken the entire week off. Things were changing around here. New investors like Vince. Although Robert hadn't formally met him, he saw Vince when he met with Roland. And now he faced his final interview process before he received the torch. He felt good. He felt great.

"Mr. Thompson. Thank you for meeting with us." The Chinese banker shook his hand with enthusiasm.

"Welcome gentlemen. Please have a seat. Let's get right down to it," Robert said.

The champagne bottles erupted all onto the floor while Drake boomed through the DJ's speakers.

"This toast right here is to success, to perseverance, and to this damn bi-polar Chicago weather," Rich said as he held his glass in the air. He was hosting a surprise day party to show appreciation for his employees and supporters to keep company morale high. His company had secured orders from retail stores from across the nation. It was a dream come true. He was blessed, he was *happy*.

Simone hugged and kissed him. "I'm so proud of you baby. I always believed in you."

"I wouldn't have made it this far without you. That's a fact. The saying is true, behind every strong man is a strong woman."

"I just love them so much!" Angelo looked at Rich and Simone in awe.

"Black love is beautiful," Marcus added as he studied the affection between the two love birds.

"Are you in love, Mr. Marcus?" Angelo asked.

"I am." He sipped his champagne to hold in his laughter from Angelo's feminine tone.

"That's good. I told Rich he need to get more handsome gay men in here. I wanna have some eye candy too, you know." Angelo giggled.

"Just keep fishing. You'll catch something." Marcus headed to the refreshments table for some fruit.

"What do you do for a living?" ChiChi asked, with a tipsy gaze. Marcus' eyes were immediately drawn to her wide hips and curvy thighs.

"I own property. And I invest."

She sucked on a strawberry. "Mmmm, I like your suit. Looking real dapper in that three-piece."

"Thank you. What do you do? I feel like I've seen you before."

"You ever been to The Pyramid?"

"Yea, I have. Rich took me there a few times."

"Well, that's where you saw me then. I dance there. And I hustle on the side."

"Oh, so you a Queen Pin, huh?"

"Whatever it takes to keep the money coming in. I ain't selling no pussy though. Fuck that!"

"Yea, I hear you."

"But we should exchange numbers though. I wanna get to know you a lil' better." ChiChi poked Marcus' stomach. Right on cue, Rich and Simone came over and interrupted the conversation.

"Marcus, you need me to call security on her, bro?" Rich joked.

"Nah, she good."

"Boy, shut up," ChiChi told Rich.

"Real talk though, let me holla at him for a minute."

ChiChi sized Marcus up before she walked off. "Ok. And I'll be back for you sir."

"She like that with everybody?" Marcus asked Rich.

"With niggas? Nah. She's lesbian, so she says, but I guess you changed her mind. But look though man…Marcus I just wanna say thank you. "

"It's no problem at all, bro. I knew your company would take off, and now look at it. I already made half of the money I invested back. That's crazy growth."

"Yea, it ain't even about the money though. You believed in me when other people wouldn't. You took a chance on me when my own father wouldn't. I don't take that shit for granted."

"Whatever it takes to be successful, I will do it. I mean that. But today is about your success. Not mine."

"I'm in your debt forever."

"No, you're not. We're partners."

Rich smiled as the two touched glasses. Marcus drank with delight, as he knew his puzzle was coming together.

ChiChi salivated over Marcus while she and Simone mingled.

"What you know about him? He looking like a whole ass meal over there, my god!"

"I don't know much about him at all. That's Rich's business partner. As far as I'm concerned, he's a stranger to me. It's something about him. I can't put my finger on it though."

"Stranger danger," ChiChi said as she undressed Marcus with her eyes.

Robert couldn't contain his emotions. He felt the tears building up in his eyes, but he kept himself in check. His hands were shaking off the Richter scale while he watched the Chinese bankers exit the room. All hopes of his father's dream project left with them. Robert had made a dreadful error in his prospectus. Too many numbers didn't add up. He screamed at his team when they were alone.

"What the fuck just happened? Now we look incompetent, and most importantly, they most likely won't finance the development now!" He threw a stack of papers to the ground in fury.

One of his advisors spoke up. "Mr. Thompson, we went over it numerous times. I'm not sure why it's not adding up on *their* end."

"I don't give a fuck how many times you went over it. It's not right. Everything is fucking wrong right now." He walked over to the window and calmed himself. The entire room was silent.

"Leave me. All of you." Everyone rushed out the door as if the room was burning on fire. But the fire was Robert. He knew his father would not like the news he had to deliver.

"Judge Thompson. I love the sound of that." Malik played in Raven's hair while she laid across her bed studying.

"Sounds good. But first I have to conquer Constitutional Law."

"I know grad school was hell, so I can only imagine how law school is. But you came this far, didn't you? You got it baby."

"I want to take a trip soon. Maybe next weekend after this exam."

Malik laughed. "Just like that, huh?"

"What?" Raven smiled in confusion.

"Nothing. I'm just saying, it must be nice to take a trip whenever, wherever. That's the life I want."

Raven sighed. "That's the life you will have. How many times do I have to tell you Malik? Money isn't everything."

"Easy for you to say. You never had to worry about it."

"Ok," Raven said with a slight attitude. She turned her focus back to her homework.

"I'm sorry. I didn't mean to upset you, boo. You right. Money isn't everything."

"Why do you continue to focus on it? Yea I have money, so what? I told you time and time again my dad is rich. Not *me!*" Her voice ascended an octave. "I have no desire to be a business woman. I have my dreams. I have goals to make my own money and make my own legacy."

"Raven, chill out."

"Why do you stress over money so much? Tell me. Do I intimidate you or some shit?"

"Nah, you don't intimidate me. It's just that I always wanted to be successful. I'm tired of bills and worrying about this and that. My mama died when I was just a baby. I grew up watching my dad and my brother work their asses off just to stay above water." Malik fought to control his anger.

Raven moved closer to console him. "Do you believe in God?"

"I do."

"Do you believe that His will is always done in all things?"

"Yes."

"I'm sure your parents are smiling down on you. I know for a fact your brother is a good man. Money doesn't solve everything. Yea, I never struggled with bills in my life, but I have struggled with anxiety, isolation, depression, and the fear of my parents never being proud of me. We all have different battles in the same war, Malik. And you are successful. You're doing great managing that property in Markham. This is just the beginning."

"You mean that?"

"Yes, I do. You're going to be everything you want to be. You will achieve everything you desire. Just don't focus on the money. Focus on you."

"I'm focused on us. I'm thankful to have you."

Raven's face lit up like a fireworks show as she smothered him with kisses.

"Tell me where you wanna go. We can book the flights now."

Malik smiled. "Well...I've never been to LA before."

Robert paced back and forth in his home office with the lights off. The darkness consumed him. The sweat grew intense. He finally mustered up the confidence to call his father and tell him what happened earlier. He had been in a daze for hours. He was hoping today was a nightmare or some sort of joke, but it was very much real. He dropped the ball, and the investors from Shanghai weren't nearly as enthused about funding this project as before.

The phone rang. His heart sped up. It rang again as he wiped the sweat from his forehead. Robert answered on the third ring.

"Talk to me son," Roland said in a cheerful tone.

"How are you, dad?"

"Enjoying this Florida sun, Robert. So, do you want to tell me about earlier?"

Robert finally realized running wouldn't save him, so he faced the music. "Some of the numbers in the prospectus were off. They weren't too happy about it, and they said they will have to re-evaluate some things."

Robert heard nothing but silence, and that spoke louder than any conversation he ever had with his father. After what seemed like an eternity, Roland finally responded.

"I see. What do you mean the numbers were off?"

"My staff made a few errors. I doubled checked and even tripled checked it, but for some reason, the Chinese are saying it's not adding up. But dad trust me. I will fix this. I *will* get that building up in the air."

"You disappoint me, Robert. You really do," Roland said in a tender voice. "Maybe I made a mistake."

"I will fix this, dad."

"I made a mistake by leaving you in charge of this. For thirty-three years, I always led the charge, and I made a mistake thinking my son would be able to handle this. And you wonder why none of you own a single share of this company yet. You're not worthy. However, you are right. That building will get in the air."

"Yes, it will. I guarantee that. Even if I have to fly to Shanghai myself."

"That won't be necessary."

"Why not?"

"Because Elliot already salvaged the deal."

That statement knocked the wind out of Robert. "Elliot?"

"Yep. He saw them leaving after your failed attempt. He offered to hear their concerns. He told them he would have an accurate prospectus to them by the end of the week, and if it matches, they will commit."

"I don't understand…How?"

"Thank you for calling me. I will talk to you after my vacation." Roland ended the call. Robert stared at his phone for a moment before he threw it against the wall with all his might.

"Dammit!" He stretched his arms against the wall and held his head down.

Leah came rushing down the stairs. "Honey, what's going on?"

"I fucked up."

"What do you mean? What's going on? You've been so standoffish ever since you came home."

"I blew the deal. The Chinese were going to retract their offer because my team and I fucked up the prospectus. But good 'ole Pastor Elliot came through and saved the day."

Leah turned Robert around so that she could look him in his eye. "Listen to me. It's not over yet. You will still win this." Leah stood on her tiptoes and kissed him. "Don't stress over it. Take a few minutes and get yourself together. I'll start dinner. The kids will be home soon."

She walked off and left Robert standing there confused and angry.

CHAPTER 15

"HE'S STARTING TO PISS ME OFF."

"I'M IMPRESSED," MARCUS TOLD HIS younger brother with admiration as he observed the new business tenants at work in their rental units. "Now it ain't just Dreams and Carl's spot. The whole property finally looks attractive now."

"Gratitude bro. I been working hard out here. Getting new signage next week. Dreer Plaza is the name."

"I see! I knew you could handle it. Now you gonna be ready for the next level." The two walked into Dreams as Izzy and EC stood outside smoking a blunt and cigarette.

"Aye fam, how many miles you get on that thing?" Izzy asked.

"Enough."

"Them damn Chevy Suburbans are gas guzzlers. But you a big nigga, so I guess you need a big car. Can't be out here driving a Chevy Spark or some shit. I like that black on black. Fifteen percent tint?"

"No. Limo," EC said. He stepped on his cigarette and went back inside.

Everyone inside watched the NCAA Tournament. The Dreer brothers took a seat at the far end of the bar. "We almost there. There are a few more pieces that need to fall in place."

"Incredible. This is a dynasty in the making. They will remember us forever," Malik said.

"Aye Malik, you see that shit? I told you North Carolina wasn't gonna make the sweet sixteen. They just took that L!" Izzy said, interrupting their conversation.

"Nigga can't you see we talking?" Marcus asked with irritation.

"My bad g. My bad I'll wait." Izzy walked back to his seat.

"What does this mean?" Malik asked.

"It means that once my plan is complete, we'll be the majority shareholders of D.T. King. At last."

"All these people thought you were crazy all these years, but you were right bro. You always been right."

"I'm proud of you man. You really stepped up since things got rolling. I wouldn't want to share this with anyone else," Marcus said.

Roland Thompson's sixty-sixth birthday party was held at the luxurious Hyatt Regency Chicago downtown. People from various backgrounds were there, including politicians, clergy, business figures, entertainers, and more. The guest list was full—everyone there to show respect to the Black entrepreneur. The entire Thompson family was in attendance minus Rich. He wanted nothing to do with his father, and he meant it.

"You should slow down. That's your third drink already," Leah warned her husband.

Robert ignored her. "Another one," he instructed the server. Robert was trying to drink away his sorrows and anger. Elliot made good on his promise and delivered a worthy prospectus to Shanghai. They agreed to finance the King's Square development. Breaking ground was set for the fall, right before Roland planned to retire.

Roland hadn't spoken a word about it or the competition between Robert and Elliot. Robert began to understand what Rich meant when he told him their father didn't care about family. Robert knew the type of man his father was, so he wasn't sure if the contest with Elliot was a ploy to get him riled up, or if it was the real deal. Either way, he was done trying to figure it out. He knew he was a great businessman.

King's Square was all over the news since the financing was secured. It was the talk of the night, and Roland received praise as expected, but Elliot was the recipient of his attention. Robert gave him a sinister look.

"Truthfully, I could remain CEO for six more solid years if I wanted to, but I believe the time is fitting right now to focus on other things," Roland explained to some of his guests.

William Sherman was nearby drinking a Scotch neat. The blackmail he endured from Marcus Dreer had taken a toll on him. He was racking his brain trying to figure out how a young boy got the best of him.

"William, come here," Roland said. As William made his way over to the circle, Roland threw his arm around his shoulder. "William has been a member of my board since '85. He can tell you what type of man I am firsthand."

"An asshole during the day and the devil at night. But he will make you rich. That's a fact," William said. The others laughed at his testimony.

"Filthy rich to be exact," Roland corrected him with a smile. One of Roland's assistants walked up to him and whispered something in his ear. His face transformed from joy to suspicion.

"Excuse me gentlemen, I'll be right back."

Roland walked off in a haste. He proceeded to a small quiet foyer in the lobby where Marcus Dreer waited for him.

"I see your assistant delivered the message," Marcus said, admiring the aesthetics around him. He turned and faced his nemesis for the first time. "*The Kings Are We,* isn't that the basis of the name D.T. King?" Marcus asked as he walked toward Roland. "Dreer Thompson King, the kings of real estate."

Roland looked at Marcus with a smug look. He knew this had to be his former partner's son, as no one knew that statement but himself and Sam Dreer. "Good 'ole Sam told you that, huh? Is that why you're here? To remind me of a pact me and my dead partner made?"

"This is a lovely venue. A very nice party. You've enjoyed a lot of success. Made millions of dollars, close to three hundred to be exact. Your family has been taken care of. You had it easy. You took all of this from my father, from my family."

Roland laughed. "Took? Little boy, this is business. In business only the strongest survive. Your dad was a visionary without a doubt. But he didn't have the '*it*' factor. He had to go."

The words added fuel to Marcus' flame of anger. "You will pay for everything. Your greed, your disloyalty, your arrogance."

"Get the hell out of my face. You're wasting my time at *my* party."

"I thought you wanted your new partner to come and meet everyone."

Roland's face went cold before he smiled. "I knew that Vince Brown wasn't working alone. So, you're the one who orchestrated all of this? Buying out my partners one by one so you can have your daddy's fair share? I must say I am impressed that you made it this far. But the buck ends here. I have a firm stranglehold on this company, and you will never be a majority shareholder. Never."

"Shareholders meeting is next month. I doubt that."

"The remaining partners will never sell to you. But let's play your little game for a second. Let's say they did in your imaginary world. It still only amounts to forty-nine percent. I control fifty-one percent of this business. I always made sure of that just in case something like this would happen."

Roland studied Marcus' face. He strikingly resembled his father. "Your father was weak, but I see you're more like me."

Marcus ignored Roland's disrespect. "I'm going to take your shares. I'm going to take this company."

Roland looked down at his foe. "You have a lot of distance to cover to catch me, and you must be out your damn mind if you think you will ever beat me."

"There isn't much distance at all. We're two feet apart. And I will beat you, Roland. Trust me. In fact, I'm going to bury you."

Marcus' stare punctured Roland. Roland stood there speechless until his assistant interrupted the standoff.

"Mr. Thompson, we're getting ready to sing you happy birthday and let you cut the cake."

"Come on Roland, it's time." Marcus walked toward the festivities, his blood boiling with rage.

Roland stood tall despite Marcus' ambush. He walked back into the hall into a warm embrace as hundreds of people sang to him in unison.

"Happy birthday to you! Happy birthday to you! Happy birthday Roland! Happy Birthday to you!"

His five-tier cake sat on a table in the middle of the floor. He made his way there and picked up the knife to cut it. He paused for the photographers from T.R.U.E Photo and then proceeded to cut the cake as everyone clapped at the spectacle. Marcus stood incognito in the rear with his hands behind his back.

William spotted Marcus and froze at the sight of him.

"What is he doing here?!" he thought to himself. He blamed himself for letting his greed blind him.

Marcus kept his eyes fixated on Roland.

Robert was inebriated at this point. He stood in one spot with his left hand in his pocket while holding his drink with the other hand.

Elliot snuck up on him. "Man, your dad sure knows how to draw a crowd, doesn't he?"

"Yea, he does."

"Are you ready to bury the hatchet, Robert? I'm over this entire conflict between us. It's not worth it."

Robert stared at Elliot. "Elliot we're co-workers, nothing more. We aren't friends. We never were. Truth is, I don't like you. I despise you actually. So, how about you get the hell out of my face and we can continue on as we've always been."

Robert guzzled down the last of his drink.

Elliot let out a sigh. "Well, I tried. I figured you would respond that way, but I hoped I was wrong. That's why I did what I did. I had to. A man with hatred in his heart like you shouldn't lead this company."

"Excuse me?"

"Your team didn't mess up that prospectus. You didn't either. I did."

"What?" Robert asked, trying to keep his composure and anger in check.

"I knew if I rigged this, your father wouldn't be happy. Then, I presented the real prospectus to the bankers a few days later. Truth is, I don't care about being the CEO. I just don't want you to have it because your emotions would ruin this company. I wasn't going to tell you this, but you had to hear it, so you can see the error of your ways. And good luck trying to tell the truth to your father or anyone else for that matter. Who will believe you? Look at you. You're drunk, and you look pathetic."

Elliot patted Robert on the shoulder and then dismissed himself. Robert had enough.

Meanwhile, Raven was networking and talking with a judge—an elderly Black woman named Edith Morris.

"We need more of us behind the bench. Not just women, but Black women. It makes me so happy to hear this," Edith told Raven.

"I'll get there. I'm not going to lose heart, trust me. I want this so bad!"

"I remember the feeling I had when I was first elected to the Circuit Court. Our ancestors were with me during that entire campaign, and they will be with you as well. Just never forget that so many have gone down similar paths to pave the way for us today."

Raven's concentration on the subject waned when she looked across the room and spotted Marcus heading out. He looked just like Malik. Was this the mysterious brother her boyfriend had been talking about all this time?

Robert fumed in the car. "That sonofabitch rigged my proposal!"

"What do you mean?" Leah asked.

"That bastard Elliot intentionally ruined my prospectus so that I would fall out of my father's grace. This piss of shit is unbelievable. I wanted to beat his ass right there in front of everyone. This shit is personal now. It's not about business or being the CEO anymore."

Leah sat in silence while her husband exploded.

"I'm tired of this shit. I don't know how, but dad needs to know the truth."

"No," Leah said.

"What do you mean no?"

"You don't need to tell your father anything. We will handle Elliot ourselves. He's starting to piss me off."

"Handle him how?"

She answered calmly. "You're going to kill him."

"Leah, what did you just say to me?" Robert couldn't believe what he just heard.

"You fucking heard me Robert. Your father has already made up his mind. Your attempt to tell him the truth will fall on deaf ears. You're a Thompson. There's only room for you at the top. When he retires, you need to be the next CEO of this company, bottom line. The only way to get this sneaky ass bastard out of here is to kill him."

Robert thought about what Leah said. She was right. Roland wouldn't believe anything, because in his mind Robert was an incompetent fool. Elliot would continue to cause problems for him going forward. He wasn't going to let his dreams slip away now, which included being the boss of his family business.

"How do we do this?" Robert asked.

"We will discuss the details at a later date, but right now, I just want you to relax and let go of all that stress."

Leah unbuckled her husband's pants and engulfed his third leg.

CHAPTER 16

"YOU GOT THESE NIGGAS ON A STRING..."

THE MOMENT RICH AND SIMONE crossed the threshold, they smothered each other with kisses. The couple tangoed out of their clothes in perfect chemistry as they made their way onto the bed. Simone's sculpted body was naked. Rich arched her back and began to fuck her with raw passion. Simone's moans echoed throughout the loft. The rain gently tapped against the large windows. The lightning illuminated Rich's motions. Simone buried her head into the pillow to keep herself quiet, but the sensation inside her was too much. She brought her head back and let out a loud squeal as her left leg stretched out and began to shake.

Following three rounds of sex, Simone laid on top of her lover as he stroked her hair.

"I love you Simone."

"Tell me why?"

"Because you support me. No conditions, no hidden agenda. You love me. That's really all I ever wanted my entire life... someone to be there for me, and I found that in you. I will make you my wife one day soon."

Simone's eyes began to fill with tears of joy. "I never thought anyone would care for me this way. Especially with me being a dancer."

"I'm not insecure about that. I never was. I trust you will never hurt me in that way."

"I feel like it's my fault you and your dad have beef. I don't have any hostility toward him, and you didn't go to his birthday party last month. I'm thankful you love me. I really am. It just sucks that I caused friction within your family."

"It's *not* your fault. Don't ever say that. My dad is a piece of shit, and we had issues way before me and you got together. Fuck him. Together we'll be better than him and richer than he could ever dream of. That's a fact."

"You promise?"

"Yes. I promise."

It was a glorious early spring morning as Marcus left Urban Capital's office to visit Rich. He walked along the busy downtown street sipping his coffee when he suddenly heard someone shouting his name.

"Hey! Hey, you. Yea, I'm talking to you, Marcus Dreer," Dion screamed with no regard for the morning pedestrians. Marcus looked across the street as Dion walked toward him with hostility. Marcus already knew why Dion showed up.

"You piece of shit. Who the hell do you think you are?"

"I assume you think I made her divorce you," Marcus responded.

"I know you did. I saw the way she looked at you. I'm aware of the history y'all got. The second I laid eyes on you, I knew you was a snake."

"Desire is a grown woman. She made her decision on her own. She chose me. I didn't force her to do anything. I have no issues with you, and I didn't snake you. We aren't friends."

"Well, I got issues with you." Dion balled his fists up as he inched closer to Marcus.

Marcus stood his ground, relaxed. "Newly hired ABC 7 weatherman Dion Lewis was caught on camera in a physical altercation Tuesday morning." Marcus paused to sip his coffee before he continued his mock news report. "It is unclear why he attacked the man, but this story is developing."

Marcus grinned. "Use your head, Dion. You're going to risk your livelihood for a woman who never loved you in the first place? She loves me, and I love her. I understand you're angry. I really do. But right now, you need to think before you react because you will regret it. In more ways than one."

Dion studied Marcus' face and laughed. "You really think you're untouchable, don't you? You're not the only one with power." Dion backpedaled slowly before turning around. Marcus watched him as he pulled out his phone and called EC.

"Boss man." EC answered on the second ring.

"How are we coming along with that homework?" Marcus asked.

"Everything is in place. Just waiting on the green light."

"Good. It's time."

Marcus ended the call and resumed his walk to his car.

Rich was working hard in the zone, undisturbed as the music roared in his office.

Marcus recited Common's lyrics as he crept up on his business associate, catching him off guard. Rich turned the music down.

"Marcus, what's good fam? Didn't know you was stopping by today."

"Yea, the workload is pretty light this afternoon, so I figured I'd come through and see how everything is going."

"We're about to launch the summer marketing campaign. Simone is the brainchild behind it. This will be epic."

"Oh yea? Simone?"

"Yep. She's the Creative Director for this project."

"How long have y'all been together, you say?"

"About a year and a half."

"You know that night we went to the club she works at, she had all the attention. She stood out like a diamond amongst rocks in there, and she wasn't even dancing," Marcus said.

"This is true. She is the best."

"I think she needs to be in front of the camera. She will hook many people, men and women. Her looks and her body are amazing. We need it all to resonate with the people," Marcus said.

"You think so?"

"I know so. Run it by her and see what she thinks."

"I'll see what she says. She was adamant about getting involved with the business side of things and not using her body as a moneymaking tool. Shit, she honestly hasn't danced in months."

"I feel you. It won't be dancing though. It's just modeling. It's no biggie, just a thought. But yea, see what she thinks."

"I'll run it by her tonight."

"This boy somehow, someway found a crack in the stone. He infiltrated the empire. The empire I built."

Roland couldn't fathom how this could have happened. "This kid has balls. I'll give him that. He has more in him than his timid father ever could dream of." He looked at William as he paced the lobby of their headquarters.

"He has some shares, sure, but he can't sway votes. He has no control, Roland. *We* are still in control," William assured the CEO, although it was a lie. William for certain was not in control of anything. He was a mere puppet.

"Luxury apartments, condos, and high rises across the country. A skyscraper on the horizon. A portfolio worth over ten billion. Sam Dreer couldn't have dreamed of this. He was happy doing fixer-uppers and penny work. Now his boy Marcus thinks he's going to come in and take it away from me? He's sadly mistaken. I have a surprise for our new partner at this month's shareholder meeting."

William was confused on what Roland meant by that.

When Simone came home that evening, Rich decided to give her the news about taking her off the creative team to become the lead model. He had made the decision in his mind. It was no longer a consideration. He believed it would be a good move, and since Nubian Noir was his only successful business, he wanted to be extra cautious.

"Hey babe," Simone said. She appeared to be in a great mood.

"Hey, how was your day?"

"It was good. Did some shopping and some brainstorming of course," she said with enthusiasm. "I know the perfect pitch for the summer marketing campaign."

"Babe, I decided to bring on a new Creative Director to help you out. He is a very bright person. I was thinking maybe you should be the lead model for this campaign's photo shoot, and then we will revisit everything after the campaign."

"I thought you said I would be on the creative team?" Simone asked.

"You are baby, but you just need some help that's all. It's all a team effort. I promise. I just think your role would be best modeling our product for now."

"So, you just pushing me back to eye candy, huh?"

"What's the issue? You been showing your body all these years and now you're above it?"

"Nigga what the fuck you just say to me?" Simone asked. Rich's words hit a nerve. She couldn't fathom what she was hearing. "Who the fuck put you up to this? Huh? That nigga Marcus?"

"Simone, calm down. He just suggested it, but I made the final decision. I think this is what's best for Nubian Noir."

"I really was looking forward to this, and you just dropped me. I quit dancing cause I wanted to build this business with you, together. Not just to be a model."

"We are building together boo, trust me."

"Never mind." She cut him off. "No worries. Fuck this shit. I'm out!" She stormed out the door.

"Simone...Simone...babe..." The sound of the slamming door cut him off.

At that moment, Rich knew things didn't go as he had planned.

Dezi embraced all of the high school girls after L.A.W.K's presentation at Wendell Phillips High School on Chicago's South Side. It felt refreshing to do something she truly loved. Her cousin Lauren waited for her in the hallway.

"The web designer said he will finally update the site this week and remove all traces of Dion."

"Ok, that sounds good." Dezi smiled.

Lauren stared at her for a moment. "What are you up to cuzzo?"

"What do you mean?"

"You divorce Dion after a year, and now you're dating Marcus again? I thought you didn't want to be with Marcus anymore."

"Dion was a mistake. A mistake I have no shame in admitting. I should have never married him and played with his emotions. I felt it was best to end it now before things got deeper. Marcus has always had my heart. I tried to resist it, but I couldn't. I really love him, and the only way to give him my all was to leave Dion."

"Mmm-hmmm," Lauren said.

"Don't mmm-hmm me. Come on, we got one more school to go to."

"I'm just saying Dezi...you sure do have these niggas on a string."

CHAPTER 17
"MORAL VICTORIES"

SINCE RICH BROKE THE NEWS to Simone, she had been staying at her condo. She had barely talked to him over the past three days. Rich was worried, so he called ChiChi to see what was going on. The news disturbed him.

"She's dancing again, huh?" Rich asked.

"Kinda, but not a lot though. She did the party Mike Capone hosted last weekend," she said.

Since Rich passed Simone over for the position he promised her, things had changed fast, and now ChiChi told him Simone had gone back to stripping. To make matters worse, Mike Capone was the man that discovered Simone years ago. ChiChi told him Capone requested a private dance from Simone, and they disappeared for some time. Rich was infuriated at this news and couldn't control his emotions.

"Iight, I'll hit you back," he said.

"Ugh, now I feel like a snitch. Ain't shit happen though, Rich. We was there for like two hours, made a quick band, and then left."

"Ok. I'll talk to you later." He ended the call and immediately dialed Simone.

"Hello," Simone answered.

"So, you shaking ass for that nigga Capone again?" Rich shouted.

"Um, excuse me?"

"I hear you was dancing at some party he threw."

"Yea, I was there. What's the issue?"

"Why are you around him? And why are you giving him private dances?"

"First of all, I have to get paid. Second of all, you don't get to question shit I do. Especially since I'm not good enough for your team. Don't worry about it," Simone snapped.

"You are a part of the team, Simone. What are you talking about?"

"Goodbye Rich. I'll talk to you later." Simone hung up on him.

Rich looked at his phone pissed. He began typing a long text message to voice his frustrations.

"Come on, poke your butt out and straighten your arm," Malik said. He was trying to teach Raven how to shoot pool at Dreams.

"I'm trying," she said in an irritated voice.

"Ok, now cock it back and hit the ball directly in its center."

Raven did as she was told and gently hit the white ball. It barely moved three centimeters.

Malik laughed. "You gotta put a little more umph into it. We're gonna work on that."

Raven turned on the TV and sat down on the couch while Malik went to the bar to get a glass of water. The evening crowd for the lounge was beginning to build up, and Malik mingled with some of the patrons. Raven loved seeing Malik at work. This wasn't her first time there but watching her boyfriend smile in his element felt relieving. He was in control. He was the boss. She knew her wealth made him feel inferior at times, but she never intended for that to happen.

"This is a nice spot, isn't it?" a random female customer asked. The tipsy woman took a seat next to Raven.

"Yes, it is."

"Have you been here before?"

"Oh yes, plenty of times. My boyfriend runs this place." Raven flashed her a proud smile.

"Boyfriend? You're dating Marcus?"

"No, my boyfriend is Malik. I call him Lameer though."

Less than an hour later, Marcus walked through the door. The security guards dapped him, and everyone seemed to know him. Raven saw him and immediately recognized him from her father's birthday party last month. Her assumption that night was just proven true. Marcus and Lameer were indeed brothers.

When Malik spotted his brother, he instantly looked at Raven from across the room with a sense of urgency. Malik thought Marcus had plans tonight. He didn't expect him to drop in randomly like this.

"What's the word tonight?" Marcus asked

"Everything's going smooth. You know, the same ole shit," Malik responded.

Marcus surveyed the crowd and noticed Raven sitting on the couch. He looked at his younger brother. The silence between them told it all.

"Do you know who that is?" Marcus asked.

"Yea, I know."

"Hey!" Raven came over and interrupted them. "Are you Marcus? The one Lameer has been hiding?"

Marcus played the role. "Guilty as charged. And what is your name?"

"Raven. I feel like I saw you at my dad's birthday party last month."

"Who's your dad?"

"Roland Thompson."

Marcus played dumb during the exchange while Malik stood there and watched.

"Oh yes, I was there. Your father and I are engaging in some business. Got something in the works."

"Wow, it's such a small world," Raven said.

"Yea, it is a small world. Well, now that everyone has finally been acquainted, Marcus let me show you the books from this week."

"No need for that bro. I was heading out and just thought I'd pop my head in. You got it. You two enjoy your night. It was nice meeting you Ms. Thompson." Marcus shot his brother a look of disdain and walked off.

"Your brother seems very, I don't know, standoffish. Is it me or is he always like that?"

"You're not the only one to say that," Malik assured her, although the truth behind Marcus' behavior tonight was due to Malik's secret affair with the enemy's daughter, which was now exposed.

Robert and Leah sat in his home office in deep thought on how to kill Elliot. The couple had been at it for a while.

"Why can't I just shoot this man and dump his body in Lake Michigan or something?" Robert asked. He was becoming frustrated.

Leah sipped her tea. "We have to keep it clean Robert. That's not clean at all. Do you want to go to jail, or do you want to be the CEO?"

Robert jumped up from his seat and paced back and forth. "Fuck! Why does it even have to come to this?"

"Life is a bitch. Survival of the fittest."

A light bulb went on in his head. "There is a quarry we use out west just outside the city limits. It's a small one. It's primarily used for landfill purposes. I can have an extra key made to access the gate. I can use the incinerator there, but I'll have to knock him out first to do it."

Leah's think tank began churning as well. "Isoflurane," she said. "It's what we use to put animals into a deep sleep before surgeries. You can put him to sleep that way."

"He's a deacon at his church. He's an integral part of the Bible study they have on Wednesday nights and usually one of the last people to leave. I would have to ambush him there."

"And you will have to take the bus."

"What?"

"You will take the bus to his church. You will wait until he comes out and then smother his face with the isoflurane. It should take about sixty seconds to render him unconscious. It'll be a struggle, so you will have to overpower him and keep the rag on his face, but that shouldn't be a problem." Leah caressed her husband's biceps. "Be as quiet as possible and throw him in the trunk once he's asleep. Then drive to the quarry in his car. Make sure you wear a hat and leather gloves."

"Once I'm at the quarry, I'll load him and his personal belongings into the incinerator along with other trash and then I'll do it, just like a cremation."

"Then, you will drive his car to a secluded location. Be sure to take the keys and discard them. Take public transportation all the way home. Keep your head down. Don't act suspicious. I'll be home waiting for you."

"Well, it looks like we got it figured out. Everything should go smooth," Robert said.

The twisted look of glee on their faces was paramount.

"So, that explains it all, huh? The nice things, the car, all of it. You been fucking the daughter of the bastard we're trying to take down," Marcus said. Malik was at his house.

"Bro, she's nothing like him. Real talk."

"I believe you. She's probably not, but she's still *his* daughter. Think Malik! How you think she's gonna react when she finds out we're taking over her family's business? How you think she's gonna act once she hears the truth that her father stole that company from dad? You know when this bastard re-wrote the articles of incorporation, he said that D.T. stood for David Thompson, his fucking middle name? Not Dreer and Thompson but David Thompson. Everything he's done was an attempt to erase our existence from that company, and now you're fucking his daughter."

"I didn't expect it to grow like this for real. We met by chance, started messing around, and we ended up here. She's a good person."

"Malik, there's so many good women out here. So many. She's just one fish out the whole sea. I don't know what to tell you bro, but the reality is y'all won't be able to sustain this fling. Tomorrow is the second quarter shareholders meeting, and we will take over that company. When that happens, y'all are going to break up eventually. I don't see how this would work long-term. Despite your feelings for her, she is still a Thompson. She may even turn on you. It's in their blood."

Malik pondered on his older brother's words. He had a decision to make—his family, or his relationship.

Marcus and Vince rode the elevator together in silence, both focused on the monumental task ahead of them. For Marcus, everything he had planned for years had come to this. It was do or die, all or nothing.

"Where did you get those cufflinks from? I never asked." Marcus broke the silence as he stared at Vince's "VB" signature cufflinks.

"Birthday gift from my grandma. Good shit happens whenever I wear them."

"Mama Brown's spirit is with us today. I can hear her now

cussing all these bastards out." The two laughed as the elevator reached their destination.

"Let's do this," Vince said. They walked into the lobby. The receptionist guided them to the main boardroom. This was Marcus' first time in the D.T. King offices. He looked around as if he was in enemy territory. He gave everyone an evil look, one of destruction, as they passed Robert Thompson's office en route.

Elliot walked into Robert's office and sat down. "So, those two hot shots are the new shareholders I assume?"

"Yea, that's them. They're into private equity. They're the ones that bought out Marid Jabbar and Jay Foster. Word is they are trying to buy everyone else out too."

"Including your father?"

"Everyone. As idiotic as it sounds, that's their plan. But it won't work. He hasn't even given me a share of this company yet. Anyway, that's not why I asked to see you Elliot. I want to make peace."

"I have no problem with you Robert. I told you that."

"I understand that. I just want to apologize for being so hostile toward you. It's not my character. Regardless of who becomes CEO, I will continue to support you and work with you. This is a family business, and if my father sees you as family, then so do I."

"I'm delighted to hear that, brother. You're one of the best business minds I've ever known. I apologize for calling you emotional. No matter what, this company has a bright future ahead as long as you're here, regardless of the position you hold."

"Thank you."

"I would love to chat some more Robert, but I have a conference call in about five minutes."

"No problem. Handle your business. We'll catch up later. You still host the Bible study at your church every Wednesday, right?"

"I do indeed. Attendance is low these days cause most people don't think about church during the middle of the week."

"I think Ima pop in one of these days."

"That'll be great. We'll be happy to have you."

Robert smirked. "Sounds good."

Marcus and Vince waltzed into the master boardroom. Roland, William, and the remaining three shareholders were already present.

"The dynamic duo. Welcome!" Roland stood and greeted them. "Mr. Brown, it's good to see you again. And you too, Mr. Marcus Dreer." Roland extended his hand, but Marcus was fixated on the pictures on the wall. All of them were the brainchild and ideas of his father, and Roland received all the credit for it.

Roland sensed Marcus wouldn't shake his hand, so he threw his arm around his back. "Gentlemen! This here is Marcus Dreer. He is the son of my original partner Sam Dreer. May he rest in peace."

Roland continued with introductions. "This is William Sherman, Bernard Howard, Dwayne Scofield, and Johnny Barron." William stood out as the only white man.

"Gentlemen." Marcus walked over to take his seat at the foot of the table. Vince sat down to his left.

"Let's get down to business, shall we," William said.

"As you all may know, Marid and Jay are no longer involved with this company. These two gentlemen bought them out via their holding company, Urban Capital. They now want to buy all of us out. They wish to control this company one-hundred percent. But in order to do that, all of us have to sell. Do any of you wish to sell to these young ambitious men."

Roland and Marcus stared at each other as the room fell silent.

"We are willing to pay full market value for what your share is worth," Vince said.

"No one is going to sell to you," Roland told him.

"Full market value, huh? You two really want this company bad," Johnny said.

Marcus nodded. "Whatever it takes."

"Well, I'll sell." Johnny's statement stunned the room, but it brought delight to the two Urban Capital partners. Marcus smiled at Roland.

"Johnny?" Dwayne asked.

"I'm tired of your antics, Roland. These trends have damaged my portfolio a lot. Now you're sinking every resource into this damn building of yours. It's not about making us richer, it's about your own personal gain." Johnny turned back toward Marcus. "We will talk about this kid."

"John, you've become a very rich man these past five years. You sure you want to do this?" Bernard asked.

"I'm sure. I've been wanting to do this, but I just couldn't find anyone with the pocketbook to take my offer. These two gentlemen have it."

Marcus continued to stare at Roland. "Well that's one in the bag. Your move."

Roland tapped his fingers on the table as he collected his thoughts. "Well, I'm sorry you feel that way Johnny. I really am. It was good doing business with you. Anyone else interested in joining him?"

The remaining shareholders shook their heads no.

"Good. Well Mr. Dreer and Mr. Brown, it's time I show you something." Roland pulled out a portfolio book and slid it across the table. "Take a look." He sat back in his chair.

Vince opened the portfolio and scanned the contents.

Roland began to explain. "Four holding companies. I'm the only shareholder in every single one. All four have ownership stakes in D.T. King."

Vince looked up at Roland in disbelief and Marcus took the

portfolio out his hands. So, these were the mysterious shareholders after all.

"If you want to control a majority stake, you have to get through me, and that is not happening," Roland said. "I admire you, I do. Valiant effort. I don't want you here, but nevertheless you found a way here, and you will remain a minority shareholder of this company until you die."

Marcus leaned back and stroked his goatee gently. "I think we are done here. We will see ourselves out." Marcus and Vince walked out of the boardroom followed by Johnny Barron.

"William, I told you that little bastard wouldn't beat me. Now it's time to put an end to this little revenge saga once and for all," Roland said, as he watched them exit.

"That bastard won?" Vince shouted as the elevator doors closed. "Even if we buy out all of the remaining shareholders, he still will have majority. It can't be over, bro. It has to be a way."

Marcus stood there in silence while Vince gathered himself.

Vince patted Marcus on the back. "Look man, I know you wanted to remove him. Shit we all did. But look at it this way. You're rich now. We all are, and we have the leverage to do whatever we want to do now. I'm sure Uncle Sam is proud of you and Malik. There's a lot to be positive about."

"You're right. We did everything we could do in the boardroom. Let's get a drink tonight and celebrate our moral victories."

CHAPTER 18

"So, WHAT DOES THAT MEAN FOR ME?"

MALIK PRACTICALLY LIVED AT RAVEN's condo now. He was barely home and only went there to get more clothes and personal belongings. He came to Raven's house nearly every day after work. He had a parking pass for the garage; the security at the front desk knew him by name, and he now had a key to her place.

Raven's house was *his* house, and that's how she preferred it. She wanted him to feel welcomed there. She wanted a future with him. Despite all of this, Malik had chills as he unlocked the door and walked in. He sat down on the couch and stared at the blank fifty-inch plasma TV screen in front of him.

"Babe, is that you?" Raven screamed from the shower.

He placed the keys on the table. "Yea, it's me." He reclined in the love seat and closed his eyes for five minutes, which felt like an eternity.

"You're here a little earlier than expected." Raven strutted past him and walked into the kitchen. The green towel covered her naked damp body while she stared into the refrigerator.

"Where do you want to go for dinner? I don't feel like going grocery shopping or cooking. I just want to relax tonight."

Malik got up and walked over to the counter across from her.

"Raven." He paused briefly. "I think we need to slow down and re-evaluate some things."

"What are you talking about?"

"I think we jumped right into this headfirst, moving a million miles per hour. I think we should slow down and think about our future."

"Our future?" Raven walked over to Malik. "What are you talking about Malik? Where is this coming from?"

"I need a break. I can't do this anymore. Not right now at least."

"A break? A break from what? From me? What did I do?" Raven raised her voice.

"You didn't do anything, trust me. I promise I just need some time alone. It's a lot going on with me right now."

"Well, talk to me. I can help you get through it. Is it about the business?"

"No. I told you I just need some time alone, and I don't want to hurt you, so please just respect my wishes."

Malik headed for the door. Raven ran ahead of him and stood in front of the door fighting back tears.

"Malik Lameer Dreer, I am not letting you leave until you explain to me what the fuck is going on with you."

"Please move," Malik said in a calm voice.

"No!" she shouted. The tears had broken through and streamed down her face. Malik attempted to hug her, but she slapped him with all of the might in her soul. Malik stumbled back without protesting at all. He knew he deserved it.

Raven began to push him repeatedly. "Why are you breaking up with me? What is going on? Is it someone else? Talk to me dammit!"

"I'm not the man for you. I'm sorry. I love you Raven. We can continue to be friends. I want that actually, but we can't coexist any longer."

After those words, Raven dropped to the floor and buried her face in her hands. Malik knelt down and kissed her on the forehead.

"The keys are on the table. I'm sorry." He walked out her condo and closed the door softly behind him. Raven's cries pounded the walls as Malik headed to the elevator, leaving a puddle of tears in his trail.

William Sherman saw the burner number appear on his iPhone screen. He reluctantly answered Marcus' phone call.

"What do you want?"

"I'm sure there will be an emergency board meeting soon. Correct?" Marcus said.

"There isn't a date for it yet."

"But it's in the works?"

"Yes. What the hell do you want?"

"At that meeting William, you will vote 'no' to everything Roland proposes."

"You know you've really fucked up my life, and you're fucking up this company!" William shouted.

"I didn't fuck your life up, William. You did. Your greed did. I'm just playing the game, so vote no. That's my only request."

Marcus hung up.

"Mike always put me at the top of the totem pole. He never passed me over," Simone fired back at Rich over the phone as the two went blow-for-blow. Rich's insecurities were getting the best of him, and his mind kept creating false scenarios.

"That nigga never gave a fuck about any bitch that shakes her ass!" Rich said.

The other end of the phone went silent.

"What did you just call me?" Simone asked. Since they started dating, Rich had never called Simone out of her name or criticized her for her profession. Rich always treated her like a queen, which was why his words hurt her so much. Had it been anyone else, she would not have cared.

Rich *knew* he fucked up. "Baby, I didn't mean it that way. Please, can you just come over tonight, so we can talk?"

"No, fuck that. You think you can talk to me any kind of way and patch it up like ain't shit happen? You need to think before you speak Richard, you really do. I don't wanna see or speak to your ass. Goodbye!" Simone hung up with a fury.

Rich tossed his phone onto his desk and shook his head at himself.

"You and Simone still having issues, huh?" Angelo asked, overhearing the heated exchange.

"Something like that."

"Boy, I'm trying to tell y'all to go to couple's therapy. Ain't no shame in that."

"At this point I'll do whatever it takes. I'm not sure if she feels the same though."

"Ima pray for y'all, but in the meantime you need to get it together. This is a big campaign we're launching. I'm about to head to the photo shoot site now."

"Yea, I'll be headed there in a lil while. Production starts at two, right?"

"Yessir."

"I'll be there."

"Ok and look alive. This is your dream, ain't it? Act like it!"

Angelo uplifted him. Rich knew Angelo was right, but this didn't seem like a dream without his woman by his side. It seemed more like a nightmare that was constantly getting worse.

Dezi's first award ceremony was a fruitful event. L.A.W.K exceeded their goal of sending twenty-five minority high school seniors to college. Thirty-seven bright young women were awarded scholarships of six thousand dollars.

Marcus admired the love of his life as she gave the closing remarks. He was happy she found something she was passionate about. The resounding applause that followed her speech confirmed his admiration. She walked backstage to where he watched her.

"How did I do?" she asked.

"You were flawless. One hundred percent."

Dezi blushed. "Thank you, baby," she said, followed by a kiss. "I really can't thank you enough for this. All of this wouldn't have been possible without your donation."

"No, this is your brainchild and your dream. You made all of this happen. I'm just the man behind the curtain."

"Ms. Winters, can we get a picture of you and all of the recipients please?" a photographer asked.

"Go on. This is your day. I'll be here," Marcus told her. Dezi took the photo op while Marcus stayed behind and made small talk with others. He suddenly got a text from his brother.

It's done.

Marcus nodded his head in satisfaction and put the phone away.

Malik, however, was at Lil Carl's. He couldn't even eat. He didn't have an appetite.

"What's wrong young blood?" Carl asked him.

"Why life gotta be so damn complicated?"

"I wish I knew. What I do know is this, my mama told me you can't worry too much about things you can't control. Just focus on what you can and let God do the rest."

"What if it's something I could control and chose not to?"

"If it's God's will, it don't matter. Everything still gonna work out according to his plan," Carl said as a customer came in to place an order.

Malik sat there and scrolled through Raven's Instagram feed.

"And you're sure it's no security camera at that church?" Leah asked.

"I'm certain, trust me. I went past it and scoped it multiple times. Also, I need to wear all black, so I'm going to buy some clothes from Target and wear them the night of," Robert said.

"Ok good. Here are two vials of the isoflurane. One should be enough, but you never know. Robert, don't be soft on him. Grab him and put the cloth over his face and hold it there like your life depends on it. Keep him quiet. He will fight at first, but the anesthetic should take hold soon."

"I got this. I used to wrestle in high school."

"That was in 1999. This is 2018."

"I have no problems manhandling you in the bed."

Leah blushed. "Focus Robert. So, no cameras at the church and no cameras at the quarry. This will be a smooth execution. The aftermath will be the true test. Don't break."

"I won't. I mean, sure dad and everyone at work will be sad, but I can play the role. Come this fall, I will be the next CEO."

Rich was livid. The footage he saw of Simone dancing and being too friendly with Mike Capone was too much to bear. She was dancing at another one of his parties.

"Over four thousand views," Rich uttered to himself as he watched the Facebook video over and over again. A phone call from Marcus finally interrupted him.

"Hello," Rich said.

"What's going on? How the photo shoot go?"

"Day one went well. We got two more days of shooting before it goes into post-production."

"Ok cool, that's great. Why you sound like someone stole your puppy?" Marcus joked to lighten the mood, but he sensed something was wrong.

"It's Simone. Ever since that day, she has been different. Real different. She's danced at two parties hosted by her ex Mike Capone. I was just watching this video and she was all over him. Like literally all over him. She hasn't spoke to me since our last argument. I fucked up. I don't know what to do bro."

"You think she's messing around with him or something?"

"I don't know man. She keeps ignoring me. I don't know, but at this point I just need to know something."

"I know a private investigator. He's very secretive and only deals with a few clients. I can have him look into some things for you if it brings you peace of mind."

"That'll be great bro. Real talk."

"No problem. I got you. I'll reach out to him first thing in the morning."

"Gratitude," Rich said.

"We will be eligible for dividend payouts in July. That will be a fat check," Vince told Marquita during their downtime in the office. After the buyout from Johnny Barron, Urban Capital became the second largest shareholder of D.T. King with a total share of sixteen percent.

"What does that mean for me?" Marquita asked.

"It means you get a raise." Vince laughed as he walked into his office. "You can leave Marquita, thank you. I'll see you tomorrow."

He put his phone on Do Not Disturb as Janelle called him back to back. She was angry he decided to work late, which meant she had to go pick up the kids. His marriage was returning back to the same old chaotic nature. But he didn't care about Janelle's happiness. His kids were happy, and that's all that mattered to him. Plus, he found solace in the business and Adjoa. He began looking at photos of his business center project and smiled as his phone continued to light up from incoming calls.

The emergency board meeting took a little over a week to get together. Roland, was accompanied by William and three other directors—Grace Chambers, a slender and tall brown-skinned woman in her mid-fifties and president of an insurance company; James Reynolds, the owner of the only local Black-owned grocery store chain; and Loretta White, an advertising executive.

"Thank you all for meeting with me on such short notice and taking time out of your busy schedules. However, we have some business to handle. I have a list of proposed amendments I wish to change in the company bylaws."

Roland passed them out to each director and pled his case. As the meeting progressed, it was time for official voting. They all voted 'yes' to Roland's request, except William. Everyone, especially Roland, could not believe it.

"Roland, these changes will hurt the integrity of the business. I suggest we edit your amendments before moving forward," William said.

"Excuse me? There is nothing wrong with these amendments and clearly no one else here has an issue with it either," Roland said.

The corporate bylaws were structured so that every vote needed a unanimous decision to pass. The directors all owed Roland a favor one way or another, so they all were at his mercy. They never challenged him.

"Let's vote again."

"My answer will still be no, Roland," William said.

"Give me a valid reason why?"

William began sweating. "I just told you."

"You're pissing me off."

William stood up. "I have had enough of this meeting. My vote has been cast." He gathered his briefcase and walked out.

"William! Come back here, William" Roland shouted as the others looked in awe.

Rich sat on a bench near the lake at the 51st beach. The cloudy overcast spring morning prevented him from looking far out into the water. All he saw before him was gray mist. The winds blew the condensation off the leaves, and the moisture kissed the back of his neck. The breeze brushed against his face as he relaxed to the sound of the waves. He closed his eyes for a few seconds to soak in the meditative scene.

When he opened them, he spotted a man out of his peripheral vision. Marcus sat down next to him holding a thick manila folder. Neither man said a word for a few moments.

"Quiet morning, isn't it?" Rich asked.

"Yes, it is. That's how I like it though."

"A city this big? Whenever it's too quiet something is wrong."

"My PI contact finally gave me some things."

"What did he find?"

Marcus didn't reply as he gave Rich the folder and looked away. Rich studied the folder's thickness and closed his eyes for a moment before he pulled out the contents. His mouth widened as he looked at the photos.

"What the fuck is he doing there?" Rich said. The first photograph showed Roland exiting his personal vehicle—a Buick Lacrosse with his KING license plate, parked outside of Simone's condo. The second photograph showed him leaving the building. "What the fuck is he doing there?" Rich repeated in disbelief. A few more photographs also showed Simone leaving.

"No signs of Mike Capone. No signs of anyone for that matter. My PI tailed her all around and found nothing out of the ordinary. But this was something worth capturing."

"Why the hell would he be over there?"

"Keep looking through the folder," Marcus instructed. "There is an audio recorder in there also."

Rich retrieved it and looked at Marcus. He hesitantly pressed play. It didn't take him long to recognize ChiChi's voice.

"Girl, listen! If you think I ain't shit, Simone is on a whole new level of savage shit right now. Her and Rich going through it and she hooked up with his daddy! Yes, that nigga got money ya hear me? He came to her crib for that pussy, and she said he invited her to his private mansion in Oak Brook next Wednesday. I ain't mad at her."

Rich dropped the audio recorder. It broke once it hit the ground. His entire body shook in hurt and anger at what he just heard.

"She isn't messing with her ex, but this evidence is strongly suggesting that Simone and your father may be involved. Nothing is concrete though. They both have been very careful. What is this private mansion stuff about?"

"Family house in Oak Brook he purchased years ago as a safe haven for us if things ever got bad. He mostly hosted parties and gatherings there. Robert and his family lived there for a year. I lived there off and on throughout the years. I never told Simone about that place because I stayed there during the height of my depression and alcoholism. How else would she know about it? This can't be real."

"I can have my guy look deeper into it if you want."

"No. He's done enough thank you. I need some time alone." Rich got up and walked away leaving Marcus on the bench.

"Rich, everything will work out. Don't forget we have to stay focused on business," Marcus said. He attempted to follow him but receded to respect his space. Had he just witnessed this type of damning evidence, he would want to be alone as well. He was worried about his partner.

Malik resisted the urge to text or call Raven. That would make things much worse. He wanted to remain loyal to his brother and the mission because he also wanted revenge for what Roland did thirty-three years ago. He, too, wanted the lavish life of wealth. But at what expense? Raven was nothing like her father, and he knew the truth. He just wished he had told her everything upfront. Perhaps things would have been easier, smoother. He sat in his small bedroom saddened over the entire situation. Izzy knocked on his door.

"Fam, you rolling with us tonight? We 'bout to head up to Bucktown."

Malik scrolled through his phone. "Nah, I ain't in the mood. I'm chilling tonight."

"You gotta shake it bro. Can't change the past. You can only focus on the future. Sitting in this room ain't going to make it better. There's more than enough women out here for an ugly nigga with money like ya self." Izzy's joked failed to lighten up Malik's mood. "Well iight g, we'll catch you later."

"Yep," Malik replied dryly. His emotions began to consume him, not just sadness but anger as well.

Meanwhile, Raven had been in bed since Malik dumped her. Her face was swollen from the crying. She was in a trance.

"I just don't understand it," she said.

Her soror consoled her. "Don't make yourself even more sick than you already are. He hasn't even attempted to call you boo. He doesn't care about you. Fuck him!"

Malik's and Raven's hearts were casualties in an invisible war fought between their families. A war that had only begun to rage.

CHAPTER 19
"How are you going to do this?"

RICH HAD BEEN SOBER FOR almost two years—fully clean from alcohol. But the recent revelation about Simone and his father had brought him to a dangerous place. In the past, he sought comfort in the bottle as a means to escape his many business failures. The business he fought so hard for was finally flourishing. He had really fucked up. He said things he shouldn't have said and fueled the downward spiral. Now here he sat on his living room floor sulking. The near empty bottle of Jameson was his only companion. Simone could be a stubborn person, but this was different.

Is she really fucking my father? The thought pissed him off even more. He threw the bottle at the wall and shattered it. He called Marcus.

"Hello?"

"Ima kill that nigga man," Rich said.

Marcus was taken aback at what he just heard. "Where you at?"

"Home."

"I'm on my way." Marcus hung up and jumped out of the bed.

"Who was that? Where you going?" Dezi asked.

"A friend of mine is going through it. Sounds like he's drunk. I need to go help him out. I'll be back in a few hours."

"I hope everything is ok."

"Yea, me too."

Marcus sped to Rich's loft as fast as he could. He walked into Rich's apartment. The heavy smell of whiskey welcomed him at the door. Glass was shattered all over the floor. Rich smoked a cigar and staggered around his place drunk, dancing to Chicago house music with another bottle of Jameson in his right hand.

"Rich?"

"My nigga Marc! You smoke, don't you? Sticks that is?"

"From time to time."

"Join me." Rich sat the bottle down and plopped his cigar in his mouth as he retrieved a Cohiba cigar out his humidor and proceeded to cut the back. He walked over to Marcus and handed him the cigar, and then lit it. Marcus puffed the stick as he looked around confused at the scene.

"Rich, what's going on with you."

"I'm relishing in reality, Marc."

"What reality? You're a businessman. You're the owner of a successful business at that. Why are you drunk? You've been clean for a long time. What's going on? Is it the Simone situation?"

Rich puffed his cigar and stared toward his window with his back to Marcus. "My father has done nothing but treat me like shit my entire life. I was always looked over. He never encouraged me, and he never supported me. I honestly don't think he ever loved me as his son."

Marcus walked up beside his associate as he continued to vent.

"Only parent I truly had growing up is my mom. My mom loved me. And this piece of shit mothafucka cheated on her. With my woman!"

"Are you certain about that?"

"The writing is on the wall. He couldn't stop me from starting my business and now he wants to ruin my relationship."

Marcus took a puff from the cigar and sat down at the kitchen counter. "You aren't the only one who feels that way. Your father ruined my family too," Marcus said.

"How?"

"D.T. King. The business that made him so rich wasn't founded by him. My father was the original founder of the company and then your dad screwed him ten years later."

"Are you serious?"

"Yes. Dreer-Thompson King was the name. Your dad erased all existence of my father's presence from the business. As a result, Rich, I've attempted to buy him out and take the company back, but your dad is very calculated. He moves carefully, and his end goal is to always come out on top to make others look stupid. So, I'm sure Roland did this to embarrass you. I'm not sure who is to blame more, Simone or him."

Rich pulled out a mini AK-47 that was converted to a hand-held pistol from under his couch. Marcus' eyes traveled to the gun and then back to Rich.

"That piece of shit been ruining lives longer than I thought. I'm sorry to hear about that. I can only imagine how that feels to have everything robbed from you."

"You don't know the half of it," Marcus said as he stared at the weapon. "In your opinion Rich, what is the strongest drug?"

"Cocaine, heroin, a full bottle. Shit, I don't know."

"Power. Power is the strongest drug. The control of people, inferior or superior. Your father has controlled your emotions for a long time. Don't let him control them anymore. Don't feed his addiction."

"I'm going there Wednesday night, and I'm going to handle this shit. I can't take it anymore."

"So, you're just going to gun him down, and then what?"

Rich ignored the question. "Robert gave me this to keep. He got more guns than the Harlem Hellfighters."

"Rich, are you serious about this?"

"Yes, more serious than I ever been. I don't give a fuck about anything anymore. Only thing I want now is revenge. After that,

I'm going to Canada. I know some people up there, and I can start a new life away from everything in solitary."

"And how are you going to do this?"

"I don't know what time they will be there Wednesday, but Ima get there early and camp out. I still have the keys. When his ass pop in, it's night-night."

Marcus knew he was too involved at this point. He had to think smart to get himself out of the jam. "I'll help you."

"Yea?"

"Yea. I won't help you do it, but I'll help you afterwards with the cover up. Meet me on the other side of the 35th street bridge near the lake after it's finished. From that point I'll take the weapon and get rid of it. Don't take your phone with you. They can track that. You will have to leave it here," Marcus instructed.

Rich nodded. "Yea, that's what I'm talking bout!"

"Keep it as clean as possible, get it done, and get out of there."

Marcus was assisting Rich in planning a murder. He couldn't believe how deep things had progressed.

"Pour me a drink. I gotta think," Marcus said as he took a long pull from his cigar.

CHAPTER 20
"EVERYTHING WENT PERFECT."

ROBERT ARRIVED OUTSIDE NEW TRINITY Baptist Church at approximately 7:32 p.m. The church was a nice mid-size house of worship. Old, but they kept it in shape. The pastor and Elliot led the charge of raising funds to construct a new building, and they recently hit their goal. Elliot used to share this news a lot at work.

As planned, Robert took public transportation for the first time in his entire life. He knelt down amid the bushes in the park adjacent to the church, sporting a black hoodie with a black skullcap, black pants, and black leather gloves. He wore a white face mask to cover his mouth and nose to shield him from the isoflurane. He took a sip from a mini bottle of Jack Daniel's he brought with him to ease his nerves.

His hands began to tremble as the reality of committing a murder finally settled in. He was about to break one of God's Ten Commandments outside of God's house.

However, it was necessary to him. Elliot rigged his chances of becoming the next CEO of his *own* family business. A position he had wanted ever since he was a boy. He wasn't going to let that happen. Likewise, he couldn't forgive his father for the competition in the first place. To feel he was unworthy was a slap in the face. With Elliot out the picture, Roland would have no choice but to appoint him as his successor. Then, he would get a piece of the ownership pie. But that would come later.

Robert spotted Elliot leaving the church, and he prepared to make his move. He took out a thick dark blue towel and carefully poured the anesthetic over it. Robert cringed under his face mask at the horrid smell and looked away to avoid it. Once the cloth was heavily dosed, he put the anesthetic back in his pocket and quietly hopped the gate. Elliot's car was about fifty yards away, and his back was to Robert. Robert sped-walked toward Elliot.

"There's no going back now," he whispered to give himself courage to go ahead with the plan.

Elliot didn't see him coming at all. Robert completely caught him off guard and wrapped his left arm around his neck in a chokehold position and simultaneously covered his face with the cloth in his right hand. Elliot tried to wiggle his way out and made muffled noises like a maimed dog. Robert restrained him and tightened his grip in silence. He pulled him to the rear of Elliot's Toyota Camry away from any light and continued his tussle. Elliot became weaker and weaker until he eventually fell unconscious.

Robert laid him gently on the ground. Breathing heavy from the slight workout, he searched Elliot's pockets for his wallet and keys. After he found them, he popped the trunk and lifted Elliot inside, placing the cloth over his face for good measure. He got into the driver seat and started the car. The passenger seat contained two books, a NRSV Bible and a book titled *House of Morgan*. Robert adjusted the mirrors and pulled off as soon as he could. The streets were clear for a Wednesday night as expected.

As Robert approached a red light, a police car pulled up beside him. Robert's hands began to tremble again.

"Fuck! Fuck!" he mumbled through his facemask. He stared ahead to avoid looking in the squad car's direction. At this point, he was guilty of kidnapping. The red light seemed to last forever, the longest red light he had ever seen. It finally turned green, and he eased off not wanting to alert the cop. Luckily, the cop turned down the next residential street. Robert turned on the radio to relax. The vocals of the Isley Brothers filled the car.

Robert sang along. He hopped on the expressway and headed to his destination. He pulled onto the dirt road and drove deep into the dumping ground area. Once there, he stepped into the heavy downpour and instantly became soaked, but he didn't care. He had a job to do.

Robert piled enough trash into the incinerator to make a bed for Elliot. The car was backed up, and he popped the trunk to find Elliot still sound asleep. He lifted him up and carried him to the incinerator a few feet away and placed his body in it. Then, he placed more debris on top of him.

Once he was satisfied with the capacity, Robert closed the door.

"It's over." He declared his final words to his opponent and then turned it on. He stepped back and watched the flames illuminate the dark. Robert didn't feel remorse, sadness, or guilt. He only felt victory. He pulled out of the quarry and locked the gates behind him once the job was finished. Robert drove to a remote area near an abandoned factory and parked Elliot's car under a viaduct. He tossed the keys into the water.

It was 10:03 p.m. He walked to the train station with his head down to avoid making eye contact with anyone. As he paid for his transfer, a homeless man reeking of urine and filth stepped in front of him and shook a raggedy McDonald's cup in his face.

"Any spare change, man? Can you please help a brother out?"

"Sorry. I don't have anything," Robert lied.

"God bless," the man said as he awaited the next person.

Robert sat down in a nice corner seat on the nearly vacant train car. He was exhausted mentally and physically. He nodded off until the train's automated voice woke him up.

"Now arriving at Damen. Doors open on the left at Damen," the speakers roared.

Robert jumped up and ran off before he missed his stop. His home was about a ten-minute walk from the station. The rain poured even harder. Despite the downpour, he continued to walk at a steady pace, not worried about being drenched. Once he made it to his block, he picked up the pace.

"Almost home," he mumbled. The minute he made it to his brickstone home, he entered the front gate, closed it, and then walked to the backyard along the side of his home. He then went through the back gate to the alley to throw his mask and gloves in the garbage. Garbage pickup day was Thursday morning, so the evidence would be gone tomorrow. After that, he went through his back gate to the yard and struggled with locking it.

"This damn gate. I need to get it fixed once and for all. Ima get it done this weekend," he said to himself. He closed it as much as he could and then walked in the house through the back door where Leah was waiting for him. It was 11:14 p.m.

"Honey!" She ran over and embraced him. "Everything went smooth?"

"Everything went perfect," Robert assured her with a smile.

"Great. Come on. Let's get cleaned up and dry."

Little did they know someone had been watching Robert all week.

A black Chevy Suburban slowly crept down the alley behind their home.

CHAPTER 21
"I ALREADY FIGURED IT OUT."

T HE STORM BEGAN AT EXACTLY 9:11 p.m. that Wednesday night. The rain beat the ground with viciousness while the thunder raged. Rich parked his car outside the exuberant neighborhood and walked four blocks to the Thompson mini-mansion. The neighborhood was asleep. The large streetlights shed light on the puddled streets. His phone in his pocket buzzed. He took his phone with him despite leaving it behind as Marcus instructed.

Surprisingly, Simone had text him *I love you.* That set him off even more. Rich's mind went wild. How dare she ignore him for the past two weeks, start an affair with his father, and then text him *I love you* on the same night she was coming to meet his father again? Rich ignored her, stuffed his phone back in his pocket, and picked up the pace. He arrived at the two story four-bedroom home. It sat on a large lot enclosed by trees and a gate. Rich walked down the long driveway.

He walked inside, turned off the alarm system, and observed the home. He hadn't been there in years. He turned on the lights on the first floor and studied the family pictures on the large mantel— Roland and his mom's wedding picture; childhood pictures of Robert, himself, and Raven; business pictures of Roland; and their family trips. He felt no emotion. Family was over now. It was just him versus his father, and he was about to end it all.

Rich raided the cabinet for alcohol and found a bottle of Scotch. He cracked it open and drank straight from the bottle. The alcoholic spirit soothed his soul. He went throughout the house and observed every room, particularly the one he slept in during those dark days of his life. He sat on the bed and opened the drawer next to it and found his old journal. The last entry was August 19, 2014.

Another day, another failure. Lord I please ask that you help me get this business started off. I please ask that you give me the strength to resist alcohol. I am not in a happy place right now. I beg you Lord please.

A tear fell down Rich's left cheek. He vividly remembered those days. He had come a long way from that period, but now he was in his darkest days ever. He took the pen and added to that entry: *It is finished, April 18, 2018.* Then, he sat the journal down on his bed and walked off, leaving the bottle of Scotch behind.

As Rich settled in downstairs, he turned off the lights and pulled out the weapon, which had a silencer on the barrel. He studied it. His mind was made up. He reset the alarm system and waited for Roland to arrive.

Rich saw car lights pull into the driveway. He jumped up and peeked out the window. It was Roland's car. His body heated up with rage, and he fell back into the darkness for his ambush. He got into position by hiding in the shadows in a small nook to the left of the front door. He waited there like a spider waiting to trap its prey in a web.

Roland entered the home and walked into complete darkness. After he turned off the alarm system, he turned on the light in the foyer and proceeded to dry off his shoes on the welcome mat. He took off his coat and walked into the kitchen, turned the light on, and searched the wine cellar.

At that point, Rich emerged from his hiding spot slowly and observed his father. Rich looked at him with full hatred and disgust.

He cheated on his mother, the woman he married and claimed to love for life. He never supported anything he did, and now he chose to take away the only woman he truly loved—Simone. Rich couldn't contain his anger anymore. He rushed into the kitchen.

"Turn the fuck around," he said with authority.

Roland turned around startled with his hands in the air. When he realized it was his son, he was in disbelief.

"Rich…" Roland said.

"Shut the fuck up!" Rich shouted.

"Son…what is this all about? Is this your idea of talking it out?" Roland extended his hand.

"You're a piece of shit. That's what this is about. It's time you answer for everything."

"Look, if this is about money, I'll give you whatever you want. I promise. Just put the gun down," Roland said in a calm tone.

"I don't want fucking money. This shit ain't about money mothafucka. It's about you and me." Rich tightened his grip on the gun. "Do you respect me? Do you respect your fucking family?"

Roland hesitated and stuttered in confusion. "W-what are you talking about? Richard, listen to me…"

Roland tried to explain, but Rich had enough. He shot his father in the chest. The bullets sent Roland stumbling backwards into the counter. Roland clutched his chest. His face was full of pain and shock. He looked up at his son with blood spilling out of his mouth.

"You're no fucking son of mine," Roland said in a weak voice.

Rich stared at him. "I've always been your son. That's the problem." Rich pulled the trigger two more times, peppering his torso with bullets.

Roland's body dropped to the floor. Lifeless. Blood everywhere. Rich stood there and looked at his body in relief. He had finally served his unloving father the ultimate payback.

Rich poured himself another drink as he waited for Simone to arrive. He closed the front door and left the foyer light on to lure her inside without any suspicion.

Simone arrived some time later and observed Roland's car as she walked toward the front door. She rang the doorbell and waited a few moments. The wind and rain picked up speed, so she instinctively tried to open the door. To her surprise, it was unlocked.

"Hello?" she said cautiously looking around. She walked into the kitchen and saw blood all over the countertops and the floor. She covered her mouth in horror as she saw Roland's dead body lying there. Then, she screamed.

At that moment, Rich came out from the shadows.

"Hey baby," Rich said, his voice monotone.

Simone turned around. "Rich!" she screamed. "Oh my God, what have you done?" She backed away from him.

He had a lifeless stare in his eyes. "I did what needed to be done."

Simone tried to run away from him, but Rich pursued her and grabbed her. Simone began to hit him repeatedly until Rich overpowered her and slapped her. She fell hard on the kitchen floor and stumbled to get up. She made it into the living room before Rich tackled her and sat on top of her. He flipped her on her back. Simone was terrified while she stared into the eyes of the man she loved, the man who had every intention to kill her. She tried to fight him, but she couldn't. He was too strong for her.

Rich aggressively placed both hands around her throat and began to squeeze with all his might.

"I can't believe you! You messing around on me with my own fucking father." Rich tightened his grip around her neck. Simone's eyes grew bigger as she struggled to release herself from his grip.

"I loved you with all my heart. I loved you!" Rich screamed as tears ran down his face. Simone began to lose strength, life, and air. She slowly went still. Her eyes locked with Rich's.

Simone Hale was dead. That ambitious girl from Dolton, Illinois who defied the odds time and time again died that night on the floor in the Thompson residence.

Rich got up gasping for air. He retrieved the gun from the kitchen and put it back in his pants. He knew he had to get out of there as soon as possible. He went through the backdoor and made his way through the rain back to his parked car.

Rich sobbed uncontrollably as he held the gun and sat on the ground in front of the lake at 11:52 p.m. Marcus emerged from the shadows and knelt down with his friend.

"You did it?" Marcus asked.

"I killed them both. Both of them are gone." Rich placed the gun to his temple.

"Whoa! Whoa, Rich what are you doing?"

"Ain't shit here for me anymore, man. I'm a murderer. Nothing matters anymore."

"Rich, this isn't what you want to do. Don't do this Rich. I'm begging you. Give me the gun, Rich. Put it down. Give it to me."

Rich wanted to pull the trigger, but he couldn't bring himself to do it. That was the easy way out. He preferred to turn himself in to the cops for his crimes, and that's what he would do. He'd rather do time and live the remaining days of his life in hell because he was already in hell. He dropped the gun on the ground. Marcus picked it up.

"We stick to the plan. You head for Canada first thing in the morning, and I get rid of the gun. Come on, let's get out of here." Marcus stood up and began to walk off until he noticed Rich was not following him.

"I already figured it out. I'm going to turn myself in, Marcus. It's over. I appreciate everything you've done to help me, but my road ends here. My entire life has been one stream of bad news. I can't even..."

Rich's words were cut off by bullets that went through his forehead. His body fell to the side. Marcus held the smoking gun in front of him and looked down at his dead associate.

"Yea," he said. "Your time is up."

Marcus walked off leaving Rich's dead body near the jog trail. The rain and blood mixed together. It was 12:09 a.m.

CHAPTER 22

"I NEVER THOUGHT IT WOULD COME TO THIS."

WILLIAM SHERMAN SAT IN HIS car in front of Dreams at 1:34 a.m. The rain continued. Marcus pulled up beside him. He and EC got out the car and walked into the lounge. EC turned toward William's car to signal him to come in. William walked into the empty lounge as Marcus turned on a few lights.

"Sit down," Marcus told William. They both sat at the bar. William didn't say a word. Marcus stared at him for a few moments and then spilled the facts.

"Roland Thompson is dead. So is his son Rich, as well as Marid Jabbar."

The statement sent a wave of fear through William, and his lips quivered in sadness. He began to weep.

"They're all dead, William. All of them."

William cried harder.

"Get him a drink, E," Marcus told EC to help calm the old man down. EC gave him a double shot of Remy Martin VSOP. "Here drink it."

"Please don't kill me. Please don't."

Marcus chuckled. "Kill you? No William, I'm not going to kill you. We still have business to handle. With Roland gone, you're the interim chairman now, correct? When the media storm settles, you will appoint me as Chairman of D.T. King and then sell me your shares. After that is done, you're moving. You have a home in Seattle, right? You're going there, and you're going to stay there. You're going to do your best D.B. Cooper impersonation and disappear. You will never come back to Chicago, and you will never speak about what happened here. Ever. Do you understand me?"

William nodded.

"Good, but there is one more thing I'm curious about. Who gave Roland the idea to push my father out in the first place? Who helped him do the things he did? I know he couldn't have acted alone. It was you, wasn't it?" William didn't answer the question. "Answer me. I handled everything I needed to handle tonight, now I just need to know this one thing."

"Yes, it was me," William admitted.

Marcus stared at him. "Good. Go home and get some rest. Tomorrow will be a long day for you. You're in charge of the business, for now at least."

"Marcus, I..."

"Get the fuck out of my sight."

William walked out of the lounge with his head down. Marcus stood with his hands in his pockets and watched William pull off into the rain. His facial expression never changed.

Robert woke up to numerous missed calls from his mother. He knew something was wrong. He instantly called her back.

"Robert!" she answered the phone on the first ring.

"What's wrong mama?" he asked, clearing the phlegm out of his throat.

"Your daddy has been gone all night. Have you heard from him?"

"No, I haven't." It was uncharacteristic of his father to not call home and let his mom know his whereabouts.

"I've been calling him all night. He hasn't answered my calls. He said he was going to talk to Rich, but I haven't heard from neither one of them. I'm worried Robert, you hear me?"

"Ok, mama just calm down. I'm going to figure this out, alright?"

"Find out Robert!"

"I will mama. Stay by your phone."

Robert hung up and called his father. It went straight to voicemail. He called his brother, but it also went to voicemail. After calling them again, he then called Roland's assistant. He hadn't heard from him either.

"Robert!" Leah screamed.

He rushed downstairs. "What?" he asked. Leah didn't say a word. She just turned up the volume on the TV and covered her mouth in horror.

NBC news was all over the Thompson mansion in Oakbrook. Police had yellow tape surrounding the property. The reporter confirmed that Roland Thompson was one of two dead bodies in the residence.

"It's your father!" Leah screamed.

A chill went down Robert's spine. He dropped his phone and kept his eyes glued to the screen. He now knew where his father was.

The CEO of Nubian Noir didn't show up to work, and it concerned Angelo. Although he couldn't get ahold of Rich, he remained calm. That changed when a couple on the news reported what they had found on the jogging trail. Angelo and the staff stared at the TV as the shaken couple described the scene, and the reporter confirmed Rich's identity.

"We are near the 35th street pedestrian bridge where the body of 32-year-old Richard Thompson was found. As of now we are unclear of who the assailant was or the motive. Richard was an entrepreneur and is the son of Roland Thompson, CEO of D.T. King. We will have more details as this story develops. Sherrie Phillips, CBS 2."

Everyone was hit hard by what they heard. Angelo immediately began to cry, but he had to compose himself. He was now the boss in wake of the tragedy. He texted Marcus, the only person he knew he could turn to.

The Thompson family had been at the Beverly house all day. A wave of grief held them all hostage. Raven's tears were uncontrollable— her father and brother both murdered in the same night. She couldn't make sense of it. Robert held his mother tightly as she wept. As a man who had just committed murder himself the day before, Robert was now feeling a double dose of death.

Detective Jones walked in the home to brief the family.

"Good evening everyone. We've been investigating both crime scenes tirelessly. So far it appears that Richard Thompson murdered Roland Thompson and Simone Hale at the Oak Brook residence located at 324 Nottingwood Drive. He then drove to the city of Chicago and was near Lake Shore Drive. We are still working on his case, and we will find the person responsible for his death. I promise."

"No! No!" Gloria shouted. "My son would not kill his father. This makes no sense." She wept as Robert embraced her. Raven's cries echoed her mom's woes while Leah held her. The entire scene was a lot to bear, but Detective Jones remained unfazed. He had witnessed this scenario repeatedly throughout this career.

"Mrs. Thompson, your husband and son were known to have a lot of hostility between them, correct?"

"Nothing that would drive him to kill his own father," she said.

"We have retrieved the footage from the security cameras, and it shows all victims arriving at different time stamps. Rich was first, Roland second, Simone third. Do you know why all three of them would be there?"

"Roland told me Rich had contacted him saying he wanted to talk things out and reason with him. I don't know why that girl was there. Maybe cause Rich told her to come. I don't know." Her voiced cracked.

Detective Jones signaled to speak with Robert alone. Robert entrusted his other male relatives to care for his mom while he stepped in another room.

Once they were in a private area, Detective Jones told Robert his theory. "Mr. Thompson, we have reason to believe that your father, Roland, had been having an affair with Simone Hale, your brother's lover. As a result, this led Richard to murder both of them."

Robert dismissed his theory and tried to keep his voice down. "That's impossible. My father would never cheat on my mother, and he damn sure wouldn't do it with my brother's girlfriend!"

"I know it's difficult to fathom right now, but all signs point to this. I'm sorry."

"So, if he killed them, then who killed my brother? Explain that."

"As I said before, we are diligently working on that and we will have someone in custody sooner than later."

"I think you and your team need to do some more digging detective."

"Will do." Detective Jones saw himself out.

Robert's emotions took him by storm, and he began crying. He had committed murder to lead his family business, but now he was the only one left in his family to lead any of it. A part of him felt this was karma's swift justice for the sins he committed the previous night.

"What have I done?" he said out loud as he cried. Leah found her husband and hugged him from behind as he rested his head on the wall. "This is my fault."

"No," Leah sternly told him. "This is not your fault. You did what you had to do. It has nothing to do with this. Only thing we can do now is pray that the person responsible for Rich's death is found as quickly as possible."

"Rich killed dad. I never thought it would come to this."

"Their relationship was very strained. We will never know what happened that night or why that girl was there. In times like this we need God."

The couple hugged. Suddenly, they heard a loud car alarm, which caught everyone in the house by surprise. Robert rushed to the door to inquire about the alarm. His car caused the commotion. He went to retrieve his keys with haste to silence it.

"Stupid ass car. That's why I only drive it to work and nowhere else," Robert mumbled.

Alerted by the unexpected commotion, one of the cops noticed something unusual on the floorboard on the backseat of the driver's side.

"Detective, do you see that?" The cop pointed inside Robert's car.

Detective Jones looked inside the car and then walked back toward the Thompson home to inquire about the items that caught their attention.

Malik had never met Raven's brother despite her countless attempts to bring him around her family. He tried to call her to give his condolences, but no answer. He tried texting her, but no response. He felt terrible. He could only imagine the pain Raven was going through. He wanted to be there for her, but he knew his face was the last thing she wanted to see right now. He didn't know the significance of Roland Thompson being dead, but he would know soon enough. Vince texted him.

You heard what happened right?

Yea man it's all over the news. It's crazy.

It's unfortunate, but this means we inherit the empire.

How?

Be at the office in one hour. I will explain.

Malik quickly jumped up and headed northbound for Urban Capital HQ. He made it there within thirty minutes. Once he entered the office, he noticed Marquita was not there. Neither was Marcus. Vince was in his private office and signaled for Malik to come in.

Malik sat down. "What's going on? Marc ain't answered my calls. Where's Marquita?"

"Marquita has the day off. Marcus is handling some other business."

Malik gave Vince a confused look.

"We won," Vince said. "The circumstances aren't ideal, but we still won. Roland Thompson structured the bylaws to state that whenever he died, his current company share would be passed down to the next largest shareholder. In this case, it is us. The transfer will take a few weeks, but it's happening. Roland's untimely death put us in this fortunate situation."

"What?" Malik couldn't wrap his mind around what he was hearing.

"Malik." Vince leaned forward. "We did it. D.T King belongs to us now. We're rich, we control it."

"Damn, we legit did this shit. We made it. We took the company back."

Malik smiled. Today was turning out to be a good day.

The mood was extremely somber at Nubian Noir. Marcus witnessed co-workers crying and hugging each other. Angelo was relieved to see him.

"Marcus, thank you for coming. This just doesn't seem real."

"I know. I can't believe it."

"What do we do now?" Angelo asked.

Marcus turned his attention to everyone in the loft office space and spoke from the top of the banister.

"As you all know by now, our leader, our friend, our partner Rich Thompson's body was found this morning. I can't even begin to describe the feelings I have in me. When I invested in Rich, I invested in him. This business Nubian Noir was his dream, his baby. I know all too well about the struggle of finding financing, and when I was blessed with the opportunity to invest in him, I did it immediately because of his character and perseverance. In nearly one year, he grew his dream into a profitable company. He created a work-friendly atmosphere. Rich wasn't just a CEO, he was a teammate. And we will truly miss him. However, Rich wouldn't want us to stop working. Not now. He'd want us to keep Nubian Noir going strong and continue to uphold the culture he created here. We cannot quit, and we will not quit. We will get through this tough time together!"

Marcus' speech lifted the office morale for a moment.

"You have a way with words, Mr. Dreer," Angelo said. "I can't believe Simone would do that to him. Fuck his father?"

"You never know what a person's true motives are until it's too late. Angelo, you're in charge now. This is your ship, and you have to keep it afloat."

"I will do my best."

"I know. You got this."

CHAPTER 23
"*THE DREAM IS REAL.*"

THE CEO WAS DEAD. THE Senior Vice President had
been missing for over a week. And now the COO was
arrested. D.T. King Properties Inc. was in a downward
spiral. William and the board were trying to keep things in order.
The company was in disarray, and everyone knew it.

Robert being arrested was the icing on the cake. He was
charged with the murder of his brother. Detective Jones and his
men had spotted the converted assault rifle in Robert's car the day
they briefed the family on Roland and Simone's murders. Robert
admitted it was his gun, but he denied placing it there. However,
assault rifles were illegal in Cook County, so the authorities
confiscated the weapon. Ballistic testing confirmed the same gun
murdered Roland and Rich that fateful night. When they came to
D.T. King offices to arrest him, the place turned in to a madhouse.
After receiving the news, Leah stormed out of her office to visit
Robert's holding cell.

"My husband did not kill his brother!" she shouted as two
officers restrained her. She wondered how they had managed to
concoct Elliot's perfect murder only to be charged for one they
did not commit. There was an overwhelming mountain of evidence
against Robert.

Robert sat on the floor in his cell and stared at the wall.

How did I end up here? How did I let things get to me so much and resort to killing an innocent man?

Robert's ambitions had consumed him and took him to a dark place—a place he never imagined. Now he sat in a cold cell facing charges he didn't commit. All he could do was hope he was granted a bond at his hearing. He couldn't ask God for help because he had already ignored Him.

Raven was numb to everything. The nightmare seemed to get worse. Her father cheated on her mother, her brother killed her father for the alleged affair, and now her sibling had killed her other sibling. She had received Malik's calls and texts, but she ignored them. Everything was just too much for her at the moment. The semester was almost over, and finals were around the corner. She could not focus on anything.

"Just so much has been happening, so fast I just…" Raven lost her train of thought as she tried explaining the gravity of the situation to one of her law professors.

"If you need some time for grieving, I won't count them as absences. I'm so sorry you are going through this," Ms. Durkee said.

"The room is spinning. Do you have any water?" Raven suddenly fainted and fell out of her chair.

"Oh dear! Raven!" Ms. Durkee screamed. She instantly checked Raven's pulse and dialed 911. Things were only getting worse for the Thompson Family.

William Sherman appointed Marcus Dreer as the new Chairman of D.T. King the following week. The bylaws allowed the Chairman to relieve all board members at will. Roland had the company set up to favor him and his power, and now it favored Marcus.

Marcus removed the other four board members much to their disdain. He immediately appointed Vince as his new Vice Chairman as well as the CEO of the company. Vince immediately made it a priority to get to know everyone and make allies within the ranks. Many of the company's long-time employees weren't too fond of the new leadership. As a result, a mass exodus occurred within a few weeks. Many people from mid-level to upper management left.

Marcus had actually hoped for this. He wanted to cleanse the business of anyone who still had loyalty to Roland. The sudden deaths were a major cause of people leaving. Elliot Briggs still had not been found. His wife was on the news pleading for anyone to speak up and say something. No one did.

The remaining shareholders eventually sold to Urban Capital after William did. Bernard initially resisted, but he eventually folded as well. Now the company had one shareholder—Urban Capital, which became the holding company over D.T. King. The ownership breakdown remained the same. Malik was named head of Asset Management. At the age of twenty-six, he went from managing a simple seven-storefront strip mall to analyzing potential properties for portfolios worth billions. He embraced his new role and knew that his lifestyle needed to change soon.

Marcus stood in the lobby late one evening after mostly everyone had left. He watched the workers replace the signage. The sign change seemed like a small win, but to Marcus, it cemented his victory and was the icing on the cake. Big bold, dark 3D letters were placed on the wall and read D.B. King Properties Inc. The company's name was changed to reflect its new ownership, Dreer & Brown. The Thompson name was erased just as Roland had done to his family's name thirty-three years ago.

Marcus noticed an issue of *Black Enterprise* magazine from 2010 that featured Roland as the "King of Real Estate." He read the article as he stepped in the elevator. Once he made it through the lobby of the John Hancock building, he stepped onto the bustling Michigan Ave and inhaled the spring air. He strolled southbound and passed a beggar. He gave him a twenty-dollar bill.

"God bless you," the man said.

"You too." Marcus waited for the walk signal to flash.

"You should have let God handle it," the man said.

"Huh?"

"Whatever it is you're battling, you should have let God handle it. Now everything you really care for will be taken away."

The man's statement confused Marcus. He felt a slight chill as he walked across the street. He stopped on the other side and lit a cigar he had in the inside pocket of his blazer. He took a couple pulls from it and looked at the magazine one more time. Roland was photographed wearing a big Kool-Aid smile with his hands wide open. Marcus lit the corner of the publication with his torch lighter and tossed it into an alley. Roland Thompson and his reign were officially over.

Malik called Raven to see how she was holding up, but he realized she changed her number. His heart dropped when he went on social media and saw that she deleted everything—her Facebook, Instagram, Snapchat. She had gone off the grid. It was over, and he felt bad because he had no way of contacting her. He and his brother had finally accomplished their ultimate goal of taking over the company their father started, but it came at a hefty price for him. He realized maybe Marcus was right. There were plenty of fish in the sea for him and he would bounce back. He was still young, and now he had the bank account he always wanted. Life was good, and Malik knew it. He also knew his father would be proud of his two sons. He deleted Raven's number and owned the loss. He now had business to attend to, and he wouldn't fail.

"Now can we move?" Janelle asked.

"We can assess the situation and the numbers in a few more months, and it can be a possibility," Vince told her.

Janelle's enthusiasm lately was more about the material things his new position could offer her as opposed to Vince being in a position that actually made him happy.

"Daddy I want an iMac!" Victor said as he rushed him on couch.

"An iMac? What you going to do with an iMac?"

"My teacher said they're made with Vibranium, so I want it."

"Oh, really now? We're going to have to see about that."

"If he gets one, I want one too," Vanessa interjected. Vince couldn't help but laugh at all of their requests. He asked Janice what she wanted.

"I want my eighth grade graduation party to be in Miami," she said. She kept her eyes focused on her phone.

"Miami? Nah, that's not going to happen. Find a place here."

"I don't want it here."

Janelle shoved her phone in his face. "Look Vince, this house would be perfect for us."

Vince became annoyed with her antics. "Janelle, we will talk about this later ok."

"Alright." She went into the bedroom. Meanwhile, he got a text from Adjoa with the heart eyes emoji.

Congrats on the new position boss man.

Thank you beautiful. When will I see you again?

When do you want to? Let's go to Hawaii soon.

Her plan sounded like music to Vince's ears.

"Make a wish," Dezi told Marcus as he prepared to blow out the candles. They held his thirty-third birthday party at Dreams. Marcus blew out the candles.

"What you wish for old man?" Sherri teased.

Marcus eyes scanned around the entire lounge. Malik, Vince, Marquita, Izzy, and EC were all in attendance.

"It's a secret but just know you're included in it," he told her.

"Shots on me. Free shots all night. Anything you want," Malik said over the DJ's speakers. The entire lounge exploded in applause.

"Success," Vince said as he raised his glass to toast Marcus.

"Yes. Success. You're now the CEO of the largest real estate firm in Chicago. How does it feel?"

"I don't know yet. It's all surreal right now. What a difference a year makes."

"I'm proud of you fam. Now we look ahead to the future," Marcus said.

"It's time. We have a lot of work to do. So many things to accomplish."

"Yes indeed. Now let me tell you about my plans."

"I'm all ears."

"The corner of 35th and State… you know what used to be there, right? A long time ago in the early 1900s."

"Come on now, who you think you talking to? Of course, I know. That's where Jesse Binga's bank was," Vince said.

"Yessir. How many Black-owned banks are in Chicago? Better yet the country?"

"Not many."

"Exactly. With you running D.B. King, I'll take full control of Urban Capital, and then *we* can become the bank so many Black entrepreneurs need."

"Heavy in private equity."

"Heavy!" Marcus echoed.

"Um, can I have a word with the birthday boy, please?" Dezi sarcastically asked Vince.

"He's all yours." Vince stepped away to entertain some patrons.

Marcus groped Dezi from behind. "A year ago, I thought I'd never see you again. And here we are back together. How did that happen?"

"Life is interesting. It's weird, but I don't care how it happened. I'm just happy it happened." They kissed each other passionately.

"Promise me you'll never leave again," Marcus said.

"I promise baby. I swear I promise."

Carl walked into the lounge with his workers carrying pans of wings.

"Who hungry?" Carl shouted. "We got y'all covered."

Marcus nodded toward the wings. "Didn't you say you wasn't drinking cause you ain't ate? Well, there you go."

"Um maybe I'll eat one wing. You know I'm on a diet," Dezi said. Her mouth salivated at the smell as Carl passed them carrying the wings. "Or maybe I'll have three."

"Yo ass is hilarious. Go eat and feed that thickness." He slapped her on the butt.

"I'll be right back." She laughed as she followed the food. Marcus was happy. He took a seat at the corner of the bar.

Malik walked up and put his arm around him. "Wake me up when this dream is over."

"We ain't dreaming no more, bro. Everything you see here is real. Everything we did is real. The dream is real."

"So, what's next?" Malik asked. "I'm ready."

Marcus pondered on that question for a moment. "Next, we become billionaires and we do everything in our power to accomplish it."

"Let's go! Let's fucking go," Malik said. The shots of Ciroc were getting to him.

"Shall we make a toast for Mom and Dad?" Marcus proposed.

"Oh, most definitely."

Marcus handed his brother a shot glass. "To the house of Dreer. May it never fall apart."

"To the house of Dreer!" Malik repeated as the two brothers touched glasses and threw back their shot. The world was theirs for the taking.

EPILOGUE
"IS THIS BUSINESS OR PERSONAL?"

M ARCUS DREER LOVED TWO THINGS: winning and payback. He began to plot his revenge the moment his father told him the truth that winter day. Marcus had anger in his heart from witnessing his mother lose a slow and painful battle with cancer. His anger boiled from seeing his father struggle time and time again, suffering from a broken heart and blackballed from the industry. His wrath consumed him, and in his mind, someone had to pay for what had happened to his family. Someone had to pay for the cancer bills and the lack of income.

It made sense to Marcus that Roland would be the scapegoat. The empire his father conceived was now ruled by a narcissistic tyrant. Marcus had to find a way in, and he did. He always had a passion for research, and through his diligent digging, he discovered William Sherman's greediness.

Businesses like Farmer's Boys Construction, LLC were shell companies William created. He used these firms as vendors for many of D.T. King's out of state development projects. He marked the prices so that he could pocket the extreme profits. He had done this for years, and he sucked the Indianapolis project dry. Roland never knew about any of it.

Marcus made himself a qualified intermediary—a fancy term for companies that hold money for third party transactions. Under the alias 'Jason Lagrange', Marcus deceived William. William placed large sums of money from his shell companies into Marcus's QI firm for other investments. When William wanted to withdraw funds, Marcus did what he was supposed to do to gain his trust. Between 2005 to 2017, the fund accumulated over twenty-five million dollars of dirty money that William attempted to wash for a rainy day. When Marcus decided to unleash his plan, there was thirteen million in the account.

A series of venomous events followed shortly after. Marcus researched the Thompson family to find a weak link in the business and the family. It wasn't long before he decided that Rich Thompson was his guy. Patience was Marcus' true challenge during this period. The discipline it took to wait for the right moment was painful. When he saw that Rich was looking for an investor, he knew it was time to strike.

Marcus ambushed William first to reveal his scheme; blackmail and extortion kept William in check. He then befriended Rich and gave him everything Roland never did. Support. Rich was a good guy, but he was also gullible, and he fell right into Marcus' hands. By using Rich and William, he was able to maneuver his way closer to the king. Based off what his father told him and what he discovered during research, Marcus knew Roland had the company set up air tight so that he could rule it with an iron first.

Marcus came in through the back door by picking off everyone around Roland. Marcus knew that Roland didn't find his family worthy enough to inherit the company in his will. Sure, he left them money in the will but not the company itself, which was why Marcus informed William to vote no at the emergency board meeting. Roland wanted to change the bylaws so Marcus couldn't inherit the business. However, he was too late.

The feud between Roland and Rich began organically, but Marcus fueled it. His suggestion to replace Simone as the Creative Director was the inciting incident. That's when EC came into play.

Eddie Charles was a shrewd man. A former marine, he was

dishonorably discharged for breaking his superior officer's jaw after a dispute. Once he was released, he started his own firm, UnderDog Security Inc. Marcus became his only client. Between his street reputation in East Chicago and the military, EC developed a strong underground network of people who could do a lot of things. He was the private investigator Marcus recommended to Rich. He had been running security for Marcus for seven years.

Marcus allowed EC to organize a team of goons to do his bidding. ChiChi was coerced into cooperating with them from the day she came on to him at Nubian Noir's celebratory party. ChiChi was involved in illegal activities, so they blackmailed her just like they did Marid. EC told ChiChi either she would work with them or go to jail, and she chose the former.

The first step was to convince Simone to attend Mike Capone's party after Rich demoted her. They knew this would trigger Rich's emotions. Step two: EC tipped off Roland's office to inform him the building Simone lived in was going on the market for sale. Marcus' father told him Roland took pride in inspecting properties that were in predominantly Black neighborhoods. When Roland inspected Simone's building, EC took a picture of him outside her residence.

The third step forced ChiChi to record a lie about a made-up affair between Simone and Roland. ChiChi didn't want to do it, but she didn't want to go to jail either. They gave her a payment of two-hundred thousand dollars to keep quiet. If she went to the authorities, they would turn in evidence of her financial theft.

Two fake correspondences were sent out: The first to Simone, which included Rich's forged signature, informing her that he would make her the lead Creative Director of Nubian Noir, and inviting her to have a romantic night at his family's guest house in Oakbrook. The second letter was sent directly to Roland's office with a fake apology note from Rich stating he wanted to make things right for a change. It included an invitation to meet up at the Oakbrook residence.

As both victims were led to 324 Nottingwood Drive that fateful night expecting to make things right with Rich, Rich was led there to believe an affair was in progress. Simone Hale was collateral damage, just an innocent soul caught in the crossfire. Marcus felt bad for her slightly. She wasn't a typical stripper. She wanted more in life and actually tried to get more. Her boyfriend, unfortunately, could not think for himself.

Marcus had no prior knowledge of the rivalry between Robert and Elliot, but the second Rich said the make-shift AK belonged to Robert, Marcus began to plot on him. That night he instructed EC and his UnderDogs to tail Robert. Through cunning ways, they were able to obtain Robert's car keys by deceiving the valet drivers of D.T. King. Once they had Robert's keys, they cloned them.

Instead of trying to stop Rich, Marcus encouraged him to kill his father and his girlfriend and rendezvous with him afterwards. At that point, Marcus had to kill him. There was no other choice. The moment Rich expired his own father was the moment Marcus won. It was a matter of clean up after that. EC and his shrewd team planted the weapon in Robert's car, placing the gun discreetly behind the driver's seat so Robert never noticed. Once Robert was at his family's Beverly home with the detective, they triggered the alarm to draw attention to his vehicle. The rest is history.

Rich was handled. Marid's brake lines were cut, and he was involved in a fatal car accident. William did as he was told and moved to Seattle. In late June, he died mysteriously. His autopsy revealed his coffee was poisoned. They had no suspects.

Rich Thompson, Simone Hale, Robert Thompson, William Sherman, Marid Jabbar, and even Elliot Briggs, inadvertently, were all sacrificial pawns to bring down Roland Thompson. All loose ends were tied.

Robert was granted bond at his hearing and hired a lawyer. He elected to go to trial. His family was broken however. Since D.B. King was under new ownership, he no longer had a job. He only had the proceeds from his own personal investments and money his father left him in his will. Raven and the rest of the family still didn't believe Robert killed Rich, even though all of the evidence pointed to him. He and his wife—his partner in the perfect crime he got away with—were smart but not smart enough to escape the maniacal moves of Marcus Dreer. Robert was determined to fight his trial to the nail. He was innocent, and he would sink every penny he had to prove it.

Raven fell into depression and failed two of her law school finals. She had never failed a test in her life. She often sat on the Chicago Riverwalk for hours in a deep trance, wishing and praying she would wake up. But she couldn't wake up from reality.

The Thompson family was in ruins, and Marcus didn't apologize for it. Marcus relished humiliating his enemies. He focused on the flip side of the coin. He gave his best friend an opportunity to use his true gifts and go forward with his mission. He allowed his brother to operate in a capacity to grow his business skills and grow into the man Marcus knew he could be. He made them all rich men. The love of his life came back after a long hiatus. Marcus had won.

Everything he had gone through for this moment was worth it. Now he had power, money, and respect. He was on top of the mountain.

Hardship molds great men and monsters alike.

Marcus Dreer had become both.

Peter Vail, a thirty-five-year-old Jewish man, fumbled through his pocket for his phone as he walked into the Tribune Tower. He was an investigative reporter, and a pretty damn good one.

"Hello, it's Pete."

"Peter, how are you? It's Dion."

"Dion my man! How's things over there on State and Lake?"

"Everything is going good. Listen, you remember that story back in April about Roland Thompson?"

Peter hurried to catch the elevator. "The real estate magnate? Yea I remember that. Very sad what happened to him. Hell, his entire family for that matter."

"Exactly. Do you know the new owners of that business?"

"Um no."

"A private equity firm named Urban Capital."

"Ok?" Peter was confused.

"A lot of things aren't adding up about this. The CEO dies. His son dies. His other son is awaiting trial for murder. Two additional shareholders die soon after that, and another executive has been missing for four months."

"Shit happens. Coincidences do exist."

"I don't think this is a coincidence, Pete. Something ain't adding up, and I've been doing some digging."

"I thought the weather was your specialty, Dion," Peter teased.

"Quit the bullshit man. I'm serious. Now we go way back to undergrad. I'm giving you a lead on something that can be big."

Peter sensed the seriousness in his voice. "Is this business or personal? What's the purpose behind this?"

"Does it matter?"

"No. No, it doesn't."

"I'm telling you I'm on to something here, and you have the resources to uncover it."

"Ok." Peter looked at his watch. "Think you can meet me at the corner of Wabash and Wacker around 3?"

"I'll be there at 2:50."

THE END